MW00897334

Infinite Positivity

A practical sales model to EARN business by HELPING your customers – not selling them

Aaron Schieving

Like everything I do, always for Raygan, Carmen, and Gage, who all give me so much which I am forever grateful for.

Contents

Infinite Positivity

— Introduction —

I am excited to introduce you to Infinite Positivity, the sales model I have successfully used for two decades with both services and products, in both B2C and B2B markets. This model is all about helping those you are selling to, leaving them and their situation better as a result of your involvement. When you accomplish what is most important to them, you earn trust and credibility, establishing the foundation for a long-term partnership of success.

If you are looking to simply meet your quota or earn your commission, this model is not for you. But if you want to have a positive impact on your customers, your sales, and the world around you, while establishing a replicable process for consistently filling your pipeline, Infinite Positivity is for you. Revenue will follow, even though it is not the focus.

I will be sharing pieces of this model with you, like a puzzle. My goal by the end of the book is to help you assemble all of the pieces so you too can benefit from this model. I have taught it to numerous individuals over the years and have celebrated their many achievements that came from it.

Please know that you are not alone on your journey to Infinite Positivity. I will provide the pieces and guidance to assemble them, and I will make myself available to help you. If I can clarify, answer questions, or help you use Infinite Positivity in a real-life scenario, all you have to do is e-mail me at aaronschieving@gmail.com.

I am very much looking forward to what follows, and I hope you are as well! It should be fun!

Also, I intentionally wrote this book to be easily digestible. We all have a million and a half things on our plates. Despite this, it is critical we invest time into our personal growth to avoid the world passing us by. You have taken a positive step in starting this book, but you have to continue now. You can do this by reading a small amount each day. You will find a lot of great quotes in this book. I will explain more about these quotes in Chapter Two – Positive Attitude, but in addition to that meaning these quotes can also serve as guideposts along the way. If time is short, you can read from quote to quote. The content between quotes will allow you to make your way through the book one day at a time – one positive step at a time. Bit sized content. The quotes are italicized to make them stand out and to help.

Of course, if you prefer to just dive in and read the book in a single sitting, you can do that as well.

Happy reading!

Chapter One

– Believe in Yourself –

Before diving into the Infinite Positivity sales model, it is important to first focus on our mindset. Michel Eyquem de Montaigne once wrote, "The value if life lies not in the length of days, but in the use we make of them; a man may live long yet live very little." You can spend your life any way you want, but you can only spend it once. So why not choose to help people? Why not choose to be positive? Those are choices you get to make.

How do you make this choice to be positive you ask? It starts with how you choose to approach the world and those around you. It starts with your confidence. Your success is directly correlated to your confidence. When you feel confident, the whole world seems to belong to you. You suddenly surround yourself with other successful and confident people, and both opportunities and success come your way with ease. Here are some ways you can develop a confident mindset.

The first step is to define your purpose. It is hard to be confident in what you are doing if you are not sure why you are doing it. What is your purpose in work and in life? Once you identify your "why," you will be more confident because you will be coming from a place of purpose.

Next you need to avoid comparing yourself with others. In almost every case, when you compare yourself with someone else, it takes the form of negative self-talk about how you are not good enough. Doing this weakens self-confidence. The only person you need to compare yourself with is the version of yourself that you want to become. That is it.

Then you focus on solutions. There will always be challenges. But focusing solely on a problem is a self-defeating practice. Instead, acknowledge that problems will arise, and when they do, focus on finding solutions. The more problems you overcome, the more confidence you will build and the easier it will be to find solutions. Experience is a great teacher.

Be sure to play to your strengths. Sometimes we spend more time making up for our perceived weaknesses than we do honoring our strengths. While I certainly agree with improving weaknesses, you might find that your confidence will increase when you play up your strengths. For example, if you are not good at math, do not be a CFO. Stick with your strengths.

While personally not a fan of the saying fake it till you make it, if you suffer from imposter syndrome, or the untrue belief that you are not good enough, just pretend to be confident. Keep embracing the idea that you are already successful. You might not be convinced at first, but eventually your thoughts will follow your emotions, and you will become a more confident person.

You must take action. Fear can be paralyzing. Ignore the voice in your head telling you that you cannot do something and take action anyway. The more you let fear hold you back, the stronger the negative voice will become. It works in the other direction too: The more you take action, the quieter the negative voice will become (I will tell you more about fear, the role in plays, and how you learn how to disarm it later in the book).

You need to take pride in your appearance. Simply when you look good, you will feel good. When you feel good, you feel confident. Wear the clothes you want to wear. Invest in how you look, and you will invest in your own success.

Focus on the positive. This one is critical. Every situation comes with positives and negatives. It is up to you to decide which to focus on. Negative self-talk and pessimism are a vicious cycle, and a drain on your confidence. Focus on your positive attributes instead of perceived weaknesses; focus on your accomplishments rather than on your perceived (or real) failures. Keep focused on what is working instead of what is not working.

Be ready. Success is part preparation and part opportunity. Study, practice, and do what it takes to prepare yourself for when the right opportunity knocks on your door. If you are prepared, you are more likely to have the confidence to capitalize on the opportunity when it presents itself.

It is also important to embrace the power of body language. Body language speaks much louder than words. When you are feeling down on yourself, change your posture: Pull your shoulders back, hold your head high, stand with your feet wide and put your hands in the air like a superhero. You will notice the new stance quickly changes your mood and boosts your confidence.

There is no magic solution that will suddenly make you a more confident or a more positive person. But when you focus on making consistent and small steps, you can transform yourself from a fixed mindset to a growth mindset. Building confidence is like building momentum: Just keep taking action and you will feel more and more confident with each positive step.

"Stay afraid but do it anyway. What is important is the action. You do not have to wait to be confident. Just do it and eventually the confidence will follow." - Carrie Fisher

Chapter Two

– Positive Attitude –

Confidence is the first piece of the puzzle along the way to Infinite Positivity, but you need something else to go along with it. That something else is your attitude. Your attitude is how you will be able to maintain your confidence.

For this topic, I want to introduce you to Jeffrey Gitomer's Little Gold Book of YES! Attitude. If you have not read it yet, I would highly recommend it as there is a lot of great content contained in this little book. We are definitely going to come back to this book and talk about it more, but for now I bring it up for one very specific reason.

Arnold Palmer once said, "It's a funny thing, the more I practice the luckier I get." As with most things, the more time you focus and devote to something the better you get at it. This goes for having a positive attitude as well.

In the book it speaks of immediate actions you can take to start on your path to a positive attitude. Let's face it, having a positive attitude does not come naturally to most people and is in fact a skill you can learn through practice. I am included in this and have had to work hard to remove negativity from my life to allow me to focus on the positive. I guarantee you it is well worth it.

In Gitomer's book, it suggests that you have to work at it a small amount each day. That practicing a positive attitude is the most important part of the positive attitude achievement process. The old saying is an apple a day keeps the doctor away; not seven apples on Sunday, or 31 apples at the end of the month.

After reading this book for the first-time a few years ago this concept of a daily dose of positivity stuck with me. I have a rule with all of my reading that at an absolute minimum you have to take one thing from the lessons learned and implement it into your daily life. This is where the Daily Dose of Positivity was born.

The day after reading the book, I implemented my Daily Dose of Positivity. I sent the team I was working with at the time an e-mail first thing that morning, and I told them...

"Your everyday thoughts and actions build the foundation for the strength of your attitude.

If you do the little things with the right attitude, the big things will follow.

When you start your morning by feeding your head with positive, it sets the tone for your productivity and your communication."

I told them I was going to be sending them a quote or a thought every morning to help with this.

I told them it was theirs to do with it what they will, but I hoped it provided them with a dose of positivity similar to a dose of caffeine from their morning coffee.

Ever since then, I have been on a mission to collect positive and inspirational quotes. These quotes have led to the compilation of multiple years' worth of Daily Doses of Positivity. I have shared my Daily Dose of Positivity freely with those I have worked with ever since. It is usually the very first thing I do every day.

I am grateful to Jeffery Gitomer and his book for this lesson, the idea it spurred leading to the generation of my Daily Dose of Positivity, and the constant reminder it has played in my life. Now, I am going to do the same thing for you. To help provide you with a positive head start on your day and to give you your apple a day. You may not have noticed it, but I ended the last chapter with a quote. That is one from the collection. As you continue through this book you will find many more. My Daily Doses of Positivity will be there for you to do with it what you will.

"If you have a philosophy of service to others, and if you have a positive attitude, then you can BEGIN to become successful and can BEGIN to take success actions." - Jim Rohn

Chapter Three

– The Greatest Enemy of Sales…Fear and How to Disarm It –

This is supposed to be a book about positivity; why are we talking about fear? Isn't fear negative. Fear absolutely is negative and along the journey to a positive mindset it is critical that you learn how to identify it, how to understand the power and control it can have over you, and how to disarm it.

Did you know that if your role is in sales, fear has probably cost you, personally, millions of dollars? If you work for a company that generates $5M in annual revenue, fear has probably cost your company tens of millions of dollars over the years. If the company is a $20M business, fear has probably cost the firm hundreds of millions of dollars over the years. And if the company does $100M annually, the total is in the billions. This is just individual companies. If we think about the sales lost across industries, or neighborhoods, cities, states, and nations, over the years and decades, we are talking about many trillions.

If you are confident and positive, you will enthusiastically and joyfully make the pitches to customers and prospects that growth requires. You will proactively pick up the phone. You will ask for referrals. You will follow up on quotes and proposals. But if you are fearful and cautious, you avoid this work, which results in the lost revenue mentioned above. You will seek refuge in less risky activities. Like e-mail. And research.

I am talking specifically about salespeople, but everyone deals with fear. It is human. We are wired to have it, and to avoid the situation that might make it come true. If you can consistently complete the simple communications that lead to fast sales growth in spite of your fears, you will stand far above the sales crowd.

That is exactly what I am going to help you to do. This chapter of the book is designed to help you recognize the common fears that impact (sales)people and to provide the tools, the actions, and the thinking techniques to overcome these fears. If you work through the tools and actions that follow – and do the work – you will find yourself selling much, much more, and fast.

"Nothing in life is to be feared, it is only to be understood. Now is the time to understand more, so that we may fear less." - Marie Curie

It is crucial to recognize that fear occurs automatically, ingrained within us through the course of our lives. Its roots trace back to childhood experiences, such as being spurned by peers, excluded from groups, or not chosen early for activities like kickball. As we age, rejection becomes more diverse, extending to romantic interests, team selections in organized sports, college applications, and employment opportunities. Whether through dismissal from a job or the absence of a job offer, rejection continues to be a recurring aspect of life.

Dealing with these forms of rejection and the fear requires...

1. Awareness of these fears and,

2. Proactive countermeasures

Anything worthwhile or good requires some effort. Let's identify and define the fears specifically, and then detail what they make us do and also what they keep us from doing.

What instills fear in us? Let's consider the prospect of rejection. The thought of hearing a "no" or facing rejection is a formidable concern that people universally seek to avoid. Rejection is inherently unpleasant and undesirable, and it is entirely understandable that nobody wishes to experience it. The aversion to rejection is a shared sentiment, as it is felt on a personal and emotional level. It is crucial to recognize, however, that when a customer declines a product, service, or the perceived value they offer, it is not a rejection of the individual presenting it. Rather, it is a decision based on the comparative assessment of what is being offered against their current alternatives. The rejection is not directed at us personally, although our perception often leads us to interpret it that way.

What about the fear of failure? The prospect of not achieving success can be daunting. Does falling short equate to being a failure? Our perception of failure often implies a permanent and irreversible stain on our professional track record. The fear stems from the belief that a single rejection from a customer will brand us as failures indefinitely. Failure, in this context, seems like a perpetual state, the antithesis of success, something we vehemently wish to avoid. However, let's reconsider this perspective. If a customer declines our product or service, does it truly signify failure? Is it an indication that we, as salespeople, have failed? Not at all. The customer is simply expressing their current disinterest in the offering. Our competence as sales professionals remains intact. Instead of viewing a "no" as a failure, it should be seen as an opportunity to move forward. It signifies success in gaining clarity and the chance to either progress to the next prospect or schedule a follow-up with the current one. The fear of failure, intertwined with the dread of rejection, acts as a tangible obstacle hindering us from engaging in the essential work of sales and, consequently, from achieving more success and happiness.

"Success is not final. Failure is not fatal. It is the courage to continue that counts." - Winston Churchill

What about the apprehension of not being liked? What if they harbor animosity towards you? This concern, akin to the preceding ones, traces its roots back to our formative years. During our youth, especially in school, we strive to assimilate. We exert efforts to secure approval, yearning for people to hold a favorable opinion of us. It is gratifying to be liked but distressing to sense disapproval from our peers. When reaching out to a customer, making inquiries about their nterest in additional products or services, we dread the possibility that they might develop aversion towards us – that our outreach might be off-putting. "I understand you're currently using another product, but you're not getting it from us. I value our collaboration, and I would be delighted to include this product in our offerings to you. What are your thoughts?" you inquire. The customer's response, "Never! You are the worst!" Does that sound rational? No. None of these fears follow logic.

The fear of humiliation is also quite prevalent. What would you communicate to your peers? How might others perceive you if you fail to retain this account? Who relishes explaining to their supervisor that the account slipped away? Who desires to inform others of the rejection we faced? It is an uncomfortable experience, and we are averse to casting ourselves in the unfavorable light of failure. Who wants to disclose to their family that we did not secure the business? What if it changes their opinion of us? How do you explain it to your children? These are the anxieties that besiege us. Naturally, any colleague involved in sales or managing sales teams is acutely aware that rejection is an integral aspect of this profession—a significant one. Your family is cognizant of it too. It is not the first "no," and it certainly will not be the last. It is not an issue. There is absolutely no reason to feel ashamed or embarrassed. You made the inquiry, pursued it further, aimed for a positive outcome. Instead, you received a negative response. So what? They are missing out on the opportunity to collaborate with you.

As though these fears are not enough, our brains create consequences for their coming true. Like the fears themselves, these consequences are shaped automatically. We are not aware of their formation, and we rarely really even think it through to the consequence. We simply avoid the behaviors that cause us to feel fear! For the fears described previously, what are the consequences? If these fears come true, there are terrible consequences that our brains will try to avoid. None of the following potential consequences are rooted in reality though. None of them have a good chance (or, pretty much, any chance) of happening, but we experience them as truth. They are in our unconscious imagination – they are not real – but for our fearful minds, these consequences are as real as the phone they make us avoid.

"He who is not every day conquering some fear has not learned the secret of life." - Ralph Waldo Emerson

Let's play all of this out. The customer will disengage, severing ties permanently if you present a product they currently are not purchasing from you; their dissatisfaction prompting them to depart, even after 15 years of working with you. Seeking a referral from a customer may cause such displeasure that, despite decades of positive partnership, they opt to discontinue the relationship. In such events, financial insecurity then comes. It is essential to recognize that these outcomes, though seemingly implausible, operate subconsciously, influencing our actions without conscious acknowledgment. The loss of this particular customer could start a domino effect, leading to the departure of others, and leaving you in a precarious financial position. The ensuing financial hardship will then prevent you from being able to provide for your family. The link between financial stability and family support is undeniable. This chain of events, although seemingly absurd, has a profound influence on our behavior as it resides in our subconscious.

Our ingrained fears and their envisioned repercussions significantly shape our actions—or inaction—daily throughout our lives. They hold authority over us, dictating our financial decisions and determining our success. However, the situation is not as bleak as it may seem. Neutralizing these fears and acting despite them is not the formidable task you may think. Shedding light on these fears and recognizing their absurdity is a swift and straightforward process. Despite the automatic nature of fears, overcoming them demands conscious effort and attention.

Before delving into these countermeasures, it is crucial to comprehend the effects of fear on our actions. To achieve this understanding, we must examine how our behavior is influenced when fear takes hold and consider the ramifications of fear on us. Given that fear operates automatically, demanding no active engagement on our part, and since our minds often generate consequences of fear largely on a subconscious level, the impact of fear on our behavior is likewise automatic. We remain unaware that fear is the driving force behind our actions. This process unfolds without conscious thought or attention; it is a reactive mechanism. Fear subtly dictates our conduct, yet this influence often escapes our awareness.

It makes us reactive, instead of proactive –

When the customer reaches out with a problem or pressing issue, it becomes imperative to address it promptly, to avoid losing their business. Moreover, it is best to refrain from seeking a referral during this interaction, a simple task that entails posing a brief question for fear that the customer may become upset and subsequently sever ties permanently.

"FEAR has two meanings: 'Forget Everything And Run' or 'Face Everything And Rise.' The choice is yours." - Zig Ziglar

It makes us e-mail instead of call or visit –

E-mail is safe. It is less intrusive, and the rejection is less personal. I've sent an e-mail; I've succeeded! Sorry. No, you haven't. You have done nothing! What are the odds the customer will even see your e-mail, much less reply?

It makes us procrastinate –

Fear leads directly to avoiding the things we know are important. It prevents action. We won't follow up on that outstanding quote as it might anger the customer. After all, they would call if they were ready to buy, right? Wrong, they are busy and not thinking about your quote.

It makes us perfectionists –

Perfection and procrastination are highly related. Often, both characteristics are present prominently in salespeople. You cannot send it if it isn't perfect! The thing is it will never be perfect. So, you will never send it. The way to deal with this is to send it when it is helpful, not when it is perfect. When it is helpful and good enough, send it. Because the distance between this point and perfection is occupied by fear! And it will always prevent you from getting to perfect.

Fear makes us behave in counterproductive ways. It makes us undermine ourselves with damaging behavior. It makes us lesser salespeople. This hurts our customers and, of course, our families. Let's talk about all the things that fear and its imagined-in-the-real-world-but-actually-real-in-our-minds consequences block us from doing.

It keeps us from communicating with our customers –

We do not want to bother them, or annoy them, or take up their time, or make them angry.

It keeps us from picking up the phone –

Most salespeople spend little time on the phone.

It keeps us from asking for the business –

We do not ask if our customer is ready to buy as we are afraid of being rejected. And asking means they might reject us. So, we do not ask, and never give ourselves a chance at a Yes!

It keeps us from offering additional products and services to our customers –

The customer might get mad at us or leave.

It keeps us from following up on quotes and proposals, and closing more of them –

Why? See above.

It keeps us from asking for referrals and expanding our customer base –

Why? See above. The tragedy here is that customers love to give referrals.

It keeps us from spending more time visiting our customers –

We think they do not have time for us, or they do not want to see us. If you ask them, they will tell you that very few suppliers visit them – for the same reason: fear! – and they enjoy seeing you.

The list goes on and on, but you get the idea. Fear is the reason there is no proactive communication that would help you sell more.

"The difference between winners and ordinary people is winners follow through despite fear while others just dream and take no action." - Calvin K. Lee

How do you disarm fear? Hopefully, you get the significance of confronting fear and the potential it holds over you. Here is a very straightforward two-step method for facing and disarming fear. First, you pinpoint the fear. What are you afraid of, exactly? It typically aligns with one of the fears from earlier in this chapter. Second, you articulate precisely what will happen if this fear materializes. So, if the customer responds with a "No," what is the actual outcome? Will it result in catastrophic consequences? Certainly not! None of these absurd scenarios are likely; however, unless we illuminate the fear and its anticipated outcomes, there is a tendency to believe that the fear will indeed manifest.

What will truly happen if this customer rejects your offer for this order? Nothing! Absolutely nothing will occur. On to the next customer! Keep in mind, a customer's refusal does not signify a permanent rejection; it simply indicates a "no" for the time being. Thus, you move forward. In due course, you come back to that customer and take another shot. When faced with situations where you are evading actions that could enhance your sales, employing these two steps brings your fears from your subconscious into reality. In a matter of seconds, you will perceive how illogical and nonsensical the fear is. Without taking such steps these imagined fears persist in your mind, maintaining a sense of reality.

This simple method is a powerful way to disarm fear on your own. All you need is your own attentive and concentrated mind, dedicated to this matter for approximately 10 seconds. After, you relax and find amusement in the absurdity of the fanciful consequences that seemed real before undergoing this process.

To close out this topic, it is important to remember the customer is afraid, too. You are not the only one dealing with fear. Customers are afraid their vendors will make them look bad to their boss, their colleagues, or worst of all, to their customers. It has happened before. If you buy from many different vendors, it has happened many times and will continue to happen regularly. The purchasing professional's mission in life is not to be made a fool of by vendors! They are afraid of letting their customers down. If we do not get our products there on time, send the wrong ones, or customize them incorrectly, they will not be able to help their customers. As such their fears are quite similar to yours, with one caveat – your customer fears losing their customers because of your mistakes. Considering that, it is a good thing you just learned an easy two-step process to disarm fear (remember first, you pinpoint the fear, then second, you articulate precisely what will happen if this fear materializes) to be on top of your game and to use this insight into your customer's fear to create value. You see what I did there?

"Fear kills more dreams than failure ever will." - Suzy Kassem

Chapter Four

– Helping Others –

So far in Infinite Positivity, we have focused on building the mindset necessary to use this sales model. We covered how best to believe in yourself, how to live and build your confidence, and how to recognize, understand, and disarm fear. Each of these pieces are critical components of the model. They establish the foundation the rest of the model will build upon. As such, if you missed any of these pieces please go back and read them. As we go through the rest of the model, you will see reminders of these pieces as they are that important.

As we move further into the Infinite Positivity model we are going to start at the beginning of the sales process - with prospecting. Before we get into prospecting using Infinite Positivity though, here is an example. A real-world example of helping those you are selling to, leaving them and their situation better as a result of your involvement. As when you accomplish what is most important to them, you earn trust and credibility, establishing the foundation for a long-term partnership of success. This example comes from the pharmaceutical industry.

Merck and Company, the global pharmaceutical corporation, has always seen itself as doing more than just producing products and making a profit. It desires to serve humanity. In the mid-1980s, the company developed a drug to cure river blindness, a disease that infects and causes blindness in millions of people, particularly in developing countries. While it was a good product, potential customers could not afford to buy it. So, what did Merck do? It developed the drug anyway, and in 1987 announced that it would give the medicine free to anyone who needed it. As of 1998, the company had given more than 250 million tablets away.

George W. Merck said, "We try never to forget that medicine is for the people. It is not for the profits. The profits follow, and if we have remembered that they have never failed to appear." The lesson to be learned? Simple. Instead of trying to be great, be part of something greater than yourself. When you help people accomplish what is most important to them, the revenue will follow, even if not immediately.

"Happiness is always attained by giving it away without expectation. Those who help others are eventually helped. You have two hands, one to help yourself and the other to help those around you. If you can lie down at night knowing in your heart that you made someone's day just a little brighter, you have something to smile about." – Unknown

Chapter Five

– Building a Foundation for Success –

What is prospecting? Author Mark Hunter defines it as an activity performed by sales and/or marketing departments to identify and qualify potential buyers. Simple enough. Prospecting is not a complex process. Salespeople often make it complex, but when done right, it is not. Think about this definition and you will see it simply means finding people who can and will buy from you. Whether you like it or not, prospecting is an activity every salesperson must embrace using a well-planned strategy. As such, this portion of Infinite Positivity is designed to help you prospect more effectively.

As we did with mindset, we are going to do the same with prospecting and establish a foundation to be built upon. To do that, like the definition above, what follows are simple pieces of information you must know about prospecting.

Let's face it – people do not use the phone like they once did. This has resulted in the emergence of e-mail and other communication tools to take its place. But communication tools have always evolved and will continue to do so. These communication tools did not cause the evolution of prospecting; rather, what caused it was a shift in knowledge. In the past, the seller had all the knowledge about their products – if the customer wanted to know anything, they needed the salesperson. The number of options the customer could choose from was limited to what the seller had to offer.

Today, with the internet and the ability to have just about anything at your fingertips, immediately, the customer has the knowledge, and along with the knowledge comes the ability to choose any number of options and companies. The customer can now ignore you because they feel you are not needed and will only waste their time. The customer feels if, and when, they are ready to buy, they can make the purchase online without ever contacting a salesperson. The evolution of prospecting is not due to the number of communication methods available, but rather a shift in who has the knowledge.

Since the customer has access to more knowledge, your role as a salesperson has changed. No longer should you be focusing on bringing awareness to your customers of your products. If they have a need for them, odds are they are already aware of them. As such, the only way to counterbalance this is by convincing the customer to have confidence in you by helping them. The greater the level of confidence they have in you, the greater the probability you will earn the business. Confidence is not something that is built after the customer has decided to buy; it s something you must establish at the beginning of the process. Without confidence, you barely have a contact. This is where and why prospecting comes in.

"The difference between a successful person and others is not a lack of strength, not a lack of knowledge, but rather a lack of will." - Vince Lombardi

After decades of prospecting to all sorts of customers, I have had successes and failures; business earned, and business lost; done some things right and done some wrong. Everyone in sales has experienced this rollercoaster ride of ups and downs. But you can learn from it. You can learn what creates the ups so you can replicate the actions and outcomes. You can learn from the downs so you can course correct to reduce the depth of the valleys. To do this, you need to recognize what you are doing to learn from it.

I cannot tell you how many times I have heard a salesperson say, "I'll prospect when I'm done taking care of my existing customers." Salespeople with established accounts are usually the guiltiest of this. They know they should be prospecting, but to them, prospecting is way down the priority list. Their top objective is to properly take care of their existing accounts. Or they think waiting for the next opportunity with this existing customer is easier than going out and finding a new customer (sounds like a fear of procrastination, doesn't it?). In these cases, these salespeople experience a lot of peaks and valleys when it comes to their numbers. If only they knew prospecting would reduce those valleys and tide them over until the next big opportunity comes. The truth is the accounts are their top priority because they do not want to prospect. They most likely think prospecting is something only the new salespeople need to do. They may even go as far as to tell others they would love to prospect, but the demands of their accounts simply do not allow any time for it. To those salespeople, tell you what – I will give you a ride in my Lamborghini once I win the lottery.

Have you ever heard the saying "one and done"? In sales, it is also known as "spraying and praying." It is when the salesperson makes a bunch of calls that wind up in voicemail or sends out a ton of e-mails via a mail merge or some type of contact list. In either case, the salesperson then sits back and waits for the phone to ring and orders to come in. Spoiler alert - nothing happens, and the effort that went into making one round of phone calls, or into mass e-mailing one message ends up being wasted. This results in frustration for the salesperson. Which turns into complaining that prospecting simply does not work. After telling enough people, the salesperson begins to believe what they have been saying. Think about it this way. If you wanted to get into shape, to shed a few pounds, would you work out once and magically achieve your desired outcome? No. You would establish a workout routine, you would create a meal plan, you would change your behaviors, and put in the work necessary to drive the desired outcomes. Prospecting is no different; it requires structure and work.

"If you go to work on your goals, your goals will go to work on you. If you go to work on your plan, you plan will go to work on you. Whatever good things we build end up building us." - Jim Rohn

Prospecting takes time and with work, soccer/volleyball practices for the kids, family time, and the million and a half other things on your plate, who has time to prospect? The argument is there are so many things going on, and there is little consistency to the day/week, that making time to prospect does not work. But prospecting is preparing for your future. If you decide you want to go on a big vacation next year, do you save for it? Do you research places to go and visit? Do you determine what activities or things you want to see? For most people, the answer to these questions is yes. Otherwise, think about the alternative – it is vacation time! The family is packed and ready to go, but you did not save any money, did not determine where you are going, did not book any flights, did not reserve a hotel, you get the point. It kind of makes you wonder what the family even packed; for a ski trip, a beach trip, or both?

If you do not make time for prospecting, you will find yourself in the same situation, but in this case when the month, quarter, or year is ending, and your numbers are not where they should be. You can bet management will get involved requiring last-minute requests and demands that ultimately require changes to schedules. This inevitably results in a reactive sales mode.

I have been fortunate to have had the opportunity to build sales teams from the ground up in my career. Each time, I have heard at least one person say, "We've made it this long without having a sales team; why do we need one now?" Think about this. Picture a company that has experienced some great growth because of having the right relationships at the right time with the right people. Several times in the history of this company they have been at a crossroads of not having enough business to remain open, only to suddenly have another big opportunity arise serendipitously. In a situation like this, the entire company may believe they could continue to live on this trend of what was nothing more than luck. This scenario happens more than you may think – usually with small companies that grow too quickly and never understand how and why their customers are buying their products/services.

My response to the question is always, "That is fantastic, but consider what we could do if we proactively, intentionally, and strategically add more big opportunities." Prospecting is no different. If you achieved sales success without doing it in the past you had serendipity on your side. Why not make that recurring and sustainable? It is easier than you think.

"The key is not spending time but investing it." - Stephen Covey

The rebuttal to becoming more proactive, intentional, and strategic is then, "If we provide great customer service to our existing customers, we won't have to prospect." Do not get me wrong - Customer service is essential, but that is rarely if ever, going to provide a steady stream of new customers necessary to sustain growth or cover those customers you will lose due to things completely outside of your control. It is fantastic to be known for great customer service, but that takes us right back to what we just covered about prospecting when you are done taking care of your existing customers.

Consider this as an alternative – if you offer such amazing customer service, wouldn't other customers benefit from what you offer? Wouldn't that add value and help them, making prospecting even easier? We will cover referrals in a later chapter, but your existing happy customers can help you get more customers and the correct time to ask for a referral is when the customer loves you.

When someone quickly finds success in a new sales role, people are quick to say how they are a "born salesperson." They have the right look. They say the right things. They were born to do this! It is meant as a compliment to the person, but to others, it is discouraging. For them to hear someone is a "born salesperson" proves what they want to believe about why they are not successful prospecting. They easily assume they cannot prospect because they are not a "born salesperson."

Sorry to let you down, but I am not a born salesperson. I am very introverted. I am quiet. I keep to myself. I do not engage in small talk. But despite all of that, I have been able to achieve much success in sales. I have also built and managed sales teams intentionally consisting of very different individuals, with different backgrounds, different skill sets, and different levels of experience. When those teams come together with all these differences that is when they are at their strongest.

No one is born for anything. We are all blank canvases with the ability to paint our masterpieces however we choose. All you need to keep in mind is that no one will paint your masterpiece except you though, so you must put in the work to do so. Being successful at prospecting does not require a set of skills only a few people possess. It requires work. It requires focus. It requires a strategic approach. It requires using the tools at your disposal. It requires that you care.

"Intentions count as nothing if we do not translate them into action." - Marsha Sinetar

Want to learn how to prospect the right way? This should not come as a surprise given where we started the book, and I told you we would come back to it throughout. Successful prospecting comes down to your motivation and attitude. The level of motivation you bring to the task at hand will determine the results you achieve. Prospecting can be difficult. Why make it harder by having a bad attitude?

Too many salespeople fail to realize how much they are impacting their sales prospecting results due to their attitudes. If you do not think a bad attitude makes a difference, ask yourself how much more you get done when you have a good attitude versus when you have a bad attitude.

This excerpt from Mike Weinberg's book, Sales Management. Simplified. should help you understand...

"Sales is a unique type of job. To do it successfully, you have to want to sell. Think about that statement for a minute. A salesperson has to want to sell. There is no way to effectively prospect for new business or penetrate a challenging existing customer if your heart is not in it. A miserable salesperson cannot represent their company, their solution, or themselves well. If their heart is not engaged, they won't fight to get in. They won't be able to woo a prospect.

They won't go the extra step to ask the hard questions, push past initial resistance, fight back hard against objections, or continue to pursue deals that seem to have gone dark.

This may come off as harsh, or even biased, but it's true: a miserable accountant can still do great work. An accountant doesn't require passion to close the books at month-end. An accountant can literally hate their job and yet produce accurate, timely, and valuable financial statements. But good luck trying to find a miserable salesperson who is bringing in new business and delivering their numbers month in and month out. You'll be looking for a long time because they don't exist. Miserable, mistreated salespeople don't sell. There are no miserable top performers in sales. Why? Because when their company's anti-sales culture gets out of control, top producers go elsewhere."

The first thing we must realize about our attitude is that it is up to each of us to determine what our attitude is going to be. Do not believe me? Go back and reread the earlier chapters where we covered how to believe in yourself, how to build your confidence, and how to recognize, understand, and disarm fear. Expecting someone to come along each morning and gift you a positive attitude is not going to happen. It is up to you to choose your attitude and then to work toward making your choice a reality.

"It is our attitude at the beginning of a difficult task which, more than anything else, will affect its successful outcome." - William James

So, how do you stay motivated? How do you prevent yourself from being a miserable accountant?

Motivated people ignore the negative voices in their lives. These might be people in the office and friends who have bad attitudes. They are out there, and if you are not careful, they will impact you. Motivated people associate with other highly motivated people. Just as there are negative people in the world, there are also positive people. You need to make sure you spend as much time with the positive people as possible. This might mean finding people outside of work because your work environment is full of toxic negativity.

Motivated people simply look for the positive in things. Positive people count it an honor to live each day, learn from others, and have a positive impact on those they meet and interact with. Positive people take great satisfaction in helping others achieve success (sounds like Infinite Positivity).

Motivated people do not worry about what they cannot control and instead focus on what they can control. They do not pass the buck to someone else but are willing to be accountable for everything.

Motivated people are continuously learning. They approach each sales call as an opportunity to learn something new, and it is the same approach they take to everything they do. The benefit of the learning they do each day is how they then use the lessons learned to improve themselves even more.

Motivated people know there will be tough times, but they know tough times do not last. They are aware they need to stay focused on the solution, not the problem.

Motivated people always view things in a longer timeframe than negative people, who dwell on the negativity of the moment they are in.

Motivated people set goals and are focused on achieving those goals, and along the way, they celebrate each positive step forward. The goals they set are designed to both motivate them and drive them to higher levels of success than others might achieve.

"Anyone who stops learning is old, whether at twenty or eighty. Anyone who keeps learning stays young. The greatest thing in life is to keep your mind young." - Henry Ford

When it comes to prospecting the key is to avoid becoming discouraged when something does not go right. Please know right now that some things will not go right, in fact, many things will not go right. And that is okay.

You must be able to withstand being rejected time and time again. No other profession gets told no, gets ignored, gets ghosted like salespeople do. It is unfortunately part of the process. But it is not a reflection of you. Keep in mind if prospecting were easy, someone would have created an app to do it instead.

Top salespeople have high levels of focus and drive. They exhibit it by the way they refuse to let a comment from a customer or even a series of bad events from a few customers or prospects dampen their enthusiasm for finding their next sale. These high achievers not only have the attitude to keep going on sales call after sales call, but they also are able within these calls to keep things moving forward. When most salespeople would say a call is over and there is little potential to secure the sale, the high performer can ask just the right question or make the right comment to re-engage the customer. This comes from experience, learning, and fully understanding the customer's needs. Are these people successful every time? Of course not. But over a period, they will put together enough wins to come out on top.

Focus and commitment come from within. It is the personal drive that moves you forward when everything else is saying to stop. Compare this to running a marathon. It does not take much to start a marathon, but it takes a runner with a commitment to finish a marathon. Running a marathon is as much mental as it is physical, and many would say that a marathon is started with the legs but finished with the mind. If you fail to believe mentally, there is no way the physical effort will carry you through.

Same thing in sales – you may know the process and you may know the product, but if you do not know yourself, you will not be successful. Your attitude is the difference.

"The greatest revolution of our generation is the discovery that human beings, by changing the inner attitudes of their minds, can change the outer aspects of their lives." - William James

Before we move on, it is important to make the most of what we just covered. I have a rule when I read a book. My rule is that at a minimum I must take one thing, one lesson learned, one key takeaway, one something - and implement it into my daily life. Ideally and usually, there is more than just one thing for me to implement. Without taking this next step to put your learning into action, the content will fade away.

Given this and based on the content we just covered in this chapter, I am going to help you accomplish this. It is simple. All you need to do is complete these follow-up activities:

– Building a Foundation for Success Follow-Up Activities –

- Look at those around you. Do you have more negativity around you or positivity? Consider reducing the negativity.

- Each Friday, take a notebook and record the three biggest successes you had during the week. Then take a moment to celebrate regardless of how small they may seem. Repeat this process every week.

- In the same notebook record the three things you want to accomplish the following week. Repeat this process every week.

- Do you consider yourself a motivated person? Would you buy from yourself? Are you focused? Why? Write down your answers to these questions.

As we progress through the book you will see follow-up activities like these at the end of each chapter. Be sure to take the time to complete these activities to ensure your key takeaways and lessons learned do not fade away.

"Intentions count as nothing if we do not translate them into action." - Marsha Sinetar

Chapter Six

– Successful Positivity –

People do not pay for average. People do not go looking for a mediocre restaurant or middling movie when they go out at night. Customers do not award the contract to the salesperson known as Mr. Average. Nobody says, "Let's give the contract to the company that will do a merely adequate job."

Do you seek out average in your life? Or do you want more? Embracing average as satisfactory has a significant impact on numerous salespeople and businesses. Settling for average should never be a goal.

I have a framed quote on my desk that I look at every day. It reads, "If you aren't going to be part of the greatest, you have to be the greatest yourself." It comes from a Busta Rhymes song and has always resonated with me.

Why settle for average? Doing so is an open invitation for your competitors to take your business. Customers are not seeking average; they aim to excel, and they prefer working with salespeople who share the same ambition.

Not scrutinizing every aspect of the products/services you offer, exploring beyond your industry, and questioning the established processes implies you are content with merely being average. Striving for mediocrity will not attract the customers you need, nor will it enable you to reach the level of success you are fully capable of achieving.

So how do we ensure average is not holding us back? It starts by challenging your thinking to develop a baseline of where you are today and a vision of where you need to go. If you want to change, you need to know your base.

"He is a wise man who wastes no energy on pursuits for which he is not fitted; and he is wiser still who from among the things he can do well, chooses and resolutely follows the best." - William Gladstone

In his book, High-Profit Prospecting, Mark Hunter outlines a series of questions to help you determine your base. His questions are broken into two sets. The first is more strategic in nature and challenges how you see yourself and how your customers see you. Answers to these will be more thought-based; but remember, it is not what you think that is vital, but rather what your customers think. The second is tactical in scope to help you better understand your process and its effectiveness. These questions are designed to help you understand what you are doing now to prospect.

Here is the first set –

"- What about your prospecting process is compelling to the customer? Compelling refers to the customer's willingness to engage and share what they truly want. Prospects will not do that unless they find you and your process compelling and full of potential to help them meet their needs.

- Does your prospecting process result in the customer having false expectations about what you sell, forcing you to spend time later reshaping them? Nothing can detract more from your customer's opinion of you than having them demand something they feel they deserve based on your comments; especially if it is something you committed to.

- Is your prospecting process effective enough to help reduce the amount of time you spend negotiating with customers? The better we prospect regarding finding and validating great potential customers, the less negotiating we will have to do to earn the sale.

- Is your prospecting process focused on sharing with the customer what you have to offer, or is it more about uncovering information about them? Prospecting that does not put learning about the customer first results in a high level of "no" answers from customers. There is no way you can be successful with your prospecting if you are chasing leads that do not have potential.

- Is your prospecting process segmented enough to allow you to uncover customer needs faster from different types of prospects than if you used the same process for everyone? Not all prospects are the same. This warrants repeating – not all prospects are the same. They may have the same buying profile, but their needs and preferences are not. The sooner you can tailor how you prospect, the more business you can earn.

- How does the customer see you and how can you help them? Remember, we are talking about how to leave the customer and their situation better as a result of your involvement; that's #InfinitePositivity. The number and different types of questions prospects ask you during the sales process are going to help you understand how they see you and what you sell. So, pay attention!

- How long does it take for a lead or prospect to have confidence in you? You know your sales cycle, right? Why not your confidence cycle? Prospecting is all about building confidence. The sooner the customer has confidence in you, the sooner you will be able to uncover and understand their needs."

"Positivity, confidence, and persistence are key in life, so never give up on yourself." - Khalid

Here is the second set of questions to determine your prospecting base –

"- Where do your sales leads come from? List them by type and percentage. Examples: referrals, website, cold calling, marketing, etc.

- What percentage of each type of lead do you go on to earn the business?

- How many outreach efforts does it take to earn each sale? Break this list down by type to include phone calls, voicemails, in-person meetings, video calls, e-mails, etc.

- How long does it take to earn a sale from the time the lead is first developed? Break these down by source: referrals, networking, cold calling, etc.

- By customer type, list the key reasons each customer tells you why they buy from you.

- By customer type, list the key reasons each customer tells you why they are not going to buy from you.

- How much time do you spend each day/week in the actual activity of interacting with prospects?

- How much time do you spend on activities preparing to prospect? Break these activities down into specific categories with the amount of time spent on each.

- What percentage of new customers become recurring customers?

- How much is a new customer worth to you in terms of revenue and profit in the first year? What type of customer is your most profitable? What type is the least profitable?

- Is there a particular product or service new customers are drawn to? Does this vary by lead type?

- Is there a time of year when prospects are more inclined to move forward or avoid making a decision?

- What is the average transaction amount for a new customer?

- What is the profit from an average transaction for a new customer?

- What is the three-year value of each new customer in revenue and profit?"

That is a lot of questions, right? Well, that's only half of them. There are more you will need to answer in addition to these to establish a solid foundation for your prospecting to then build a successful strategy to achieve your goals.

"Acknowledging the good that you already have in your life is the foundation for all abundance." - Eckhart Tolle

Let's get into the second half of the tactical questions about your prospecting to help you establish your base.

"- Does the customer have to buy, or is what they are buying purely discretionary?

- What are the customer's options should they decide not to buy from you?

- Is every new customer for you a lost customer for someone else?

- Is the customer's buying decision of critical importance to them?

- What percentage of your prospects come to you via referrals?

- What is the earned business ratio of those who come to you via referral?

- What percentage of your customers are experiencing your product/industry for the first time?

- How much of a financial impact does buying from you have on the customer? Consider this regarding cash flow, flexibility resources, etc.

- Is the customer's buying decision geared toward preventing a problem or enhancing an opportunity?

- When does the prospect first bring up the cost/pricing?

- How long does the average customer remain your customer?

- Do most of your new customers buy a similar item/service from you again? How long until they do so?

- What is the "after purchase" relationship like with your customer?

- How knowledgeable is the average prospect about your industry and what you sell when you first contact them?

- How well can you profile your typical customer, and does this allow you to know better how to target them?"

It is vital you establish a solid foundation for your prospecting to build upon to achieve a successful strategy to achieve your goals. That is where all these questions come into play. Use them as a guide to help you do this.

The alternative is trying to take on the universe in its entirety. This is a daunting task I have seen many salespeople struggle with and ultimately result in their failure. There is a much easier way.

Do you know the best way to eat a whale?

Whales are big, just like the universe.

Think about it.

What is the best way to accomplish this?

You do so one bite at a time. The same goes for understanding the universe and how to maximize your prospecting efforts. One bite at a time.

Bon Appetit!

"If you want to be an innovator, either in your business or in your personal life, you've got to be willing to take small steps every day. Not big leaps, but small steps." - Adam Markel

Effective prospecting requires that you have a process; one that fits you and your target market(s). As mentioned previously, not all prospects are the same. On top of this, not all businesses and the products or services they offer are the same. This is why you see all these questions - there is no one-size-fits-all solution. It is up to you to determine what makes the most sense for your prospecting and your business/products. These questions will guide you to your specific process.

Here are a few more questions you need to answer before proceeding:

- Do you sell consumables or something people buy routinely?

- Is what you sell considered a routine purchase, a capital expenditure, and/or a major expense?

- Are your customers professional buyers who work with numerous salespeople?

- If the customer chooses not to buy from you, are they buying from your competitor, or not purchasing at all?

- Are your prospects currently buying what you sell from someone else?

- Are customers familiar with what you sell or is it something you need to educate them about?

- Is what you sell purchased via a contract, quote, or some other type of deadline process?

Why should you answer these questions? Let's go through each of these so you can understand what they mean, the value that comes from asking them, and how to use them to your advantage as part of Infinite Positivity.

Do you sell consumables or something people buy routinely? If the customer is buying something routinely, you should be reaching out to them at a similar frequency; it could be as often as several times a week depending on what you sell. As an example, if you are selling food and ingredients, your prospects may easily be making buying decisions daily, so contacting them two, three, or even four times per week may not be excessive at all. Conversely, if you are selling something customers only buy on an annual basis, your frequency of contact should take that into account. For example, if you sell income tax software, it is typically something people only need once a year (in April every year) so contacting your customer in June or July will not be as effective as contacting them in January or February.

"Time is like oxygen – there's a minimum amount that's necessary for survival. And it takes quantity as well as quality to develop warm and caring relationships." - Armand Nicholi

Let's continue working our way through the questions.

Is what you sell considered a routine purchase or a capital expenditure/major expense? Products considered as routine purchases will typically not come with a robust approval process for a customer to move forward. It most likely means obtaining approvals from various department stakeholders will not be required. It likely also means the person responsible for buying may be lower in the organization and that the sales cycle is relatively short.

If on the other hand what you are selling is considered a major expenditure (e.g. capital purchase), it can mean going through multiple decision-makers to earn the sale. In this case, you will need to build your prospecting strategy around establishing relationships with multiple people in various departments at the same company. Additionally, if it is a capital expenditure it most likely means it is in the annual budget plan, which may lengthen the prospecting process to months rather than weeks.

A great example of a major expenditure would be selling processing reagents for the manufacturing of a pharmaceutical product - you will find the decision-making process involves lots of people from different departments (Quality, Operations, Purchasing, Management, etc.) and can extend over several months (six months to a year, or longer), because the customer places a tremendous weight on making the right decision rather than just making one as they must take patient safety into account.

A good rule of thumb to differentiate between routine and major expenses that I have always used is $10,000. If the total transaction is above this amount the approval process is typically more complicated and the length of time to obtain approval will reflect that. If it is less, then the process should be easier and the associated timeline quicker.

Are your customers professional buyers who work with numerous salespeople? If you are prospecting professional buyers, you are dealing with people who know how to best use salespeople. Much like you have been taught how to sell and why you are reading this now so you can learn how to sell more effectively, they have done the same. They are trained professionals who pride themselves on their work. This means they will most likely ignore your prospecting efforts until they are at the point of making a buying decision. Notice I did not say they would not receive your efforts, or they would outright delete them without consideration.

Their silence does not mean you do not prospect to them. No, it means consistency is key because professional buyers do not want to work with people they do not have confidence in. Few prospecting activities will build more confidence than consistency. Sprinkle in adding something valuable to them and over time these can become some of your greatest relationships. You just have to work hard to earn them.

"If I am going to learn and grow, I must know what questions to ask and how to apply the answers to my life. Listening has taught me a lot more than talking." - John C. Maxwell

If the customer chooses not to buy from you, are they buying from your competitor, or not purchasing at all? If the prospect is buying either from you or your competitor, it means your prospecting process must be frequent enough to allow you to be on the front end of the buying process. This means you must place a strong emphasis on developing relationships over time and educating the customer along the way. Even if they are buying from your competitor today, as long as you stay top-of-mind with the customer you will at some point have an opportunity to help them. Without the relationship and frequent contact, your opportunity will not come though. Just make sure you are ready to walk through the door opportunity opens when it comes as it may not remain open long.

Are your prospects currently buying what you sell from someone else? This is typically the hardest type of customer to prospect as they do not have a current need. With the customer already buying from someone else, it means your prospecting efforts are geared toward creating awareness. Short of having a significant point of difference, you are typically waiting for the incumbent to stumble, for your opportunity door to open. The upside is when you are successful in gaining this customer, they will most likely become a loyal, long-term customer because you will probably be helping them out of a bad situation.

Do not view these types of customers as not being worthy of your prospecting time. Invariably, the competitor that currently has the account will at some point make a mistake or have an issue. If you have taken the time to build awareness, establish the relationship, and remain top-of-mind, you could be the one the customer turns to when the existing supplier slips up.

Are customers familiar with what you sell or is it something you need to educate them about? If the people you are talking with are not familiar with how you can help them, your prospecting process must include enough time to educate the customer on your products and their value add. An example is when Apple rolled out its first smartphone. People who were sold on the Apple ecosystem were quick to adopt the phone, but for many people there was hesitancy because they did not know how the smartphone could help them. This is common with new technology and known as early adopter rates.

"Opportunity often comes disguised in the form of misfortune or temporary defeat." - N. Hill

Is what you sell purchased via a contract, quote, or some other type of deadline process? Customers who use this approach will actively engage with multiple companies at the same time, only to play the companies against each other. Too many salespeople do not understand this. As such, they will have what they think is a great pipeline, only to have it go bust time and time again. These customers also require long lead times (maybe even as many as several years) due to the length and size of some contracts. This does not mean you cannot earn good business from this type of customer.

Your prospecting efforts here must be two-fold. First, you want to find out their timeline, and second, you want to build your credibility. Your sole objective is to be on the front end of the process and not the one invited at the last minute. Your prospecting is going to take place over a long period with multiple contacts in the same organization. If you are involved early in the process, you have a much better chance to earn the business than if you are tardy to the party.

Ever heard of the rule of three when it comes to buying? It is a common practice used by many companies that require the purchasing/sourcing team to solicit at least three quotes. If you have been involved from the beginning and are the first to provide a quote, you will have the opportunity to articulate the value you bring. Those submitting second and third often are not afforded the same courtesy. It pays to be first with this type of customer.

All these questions should be pointing you to the fact that the prospecting process you develop must fit your market, your customers, and your products and/or services. You cannot just copy what someone else does. You cannot just shoot from the hip and hope for a positive outcome. You cannot expect anyone else to do this work for you. Only you can answer these questions for you.

These questions are designed to provide you with the necessary insights and guidance to help you build a prospecting plan that best suits you and what you want to accomplish.

"There is no more noble occupation in the world than to assist another human being – to help someone succeed." - Alan Loy McGinnis

Even when you have established a prospecting process, it is crucial to acknowledge there will still be variations. You will encounter outcomes that are not what they could or should be. Although it requires additional time to tailor your approach based on the specific customer type, doing so will lead to more success. You must slow down to speed up.

Every salesperson should have an overall prospecting plan (on paper). It is also advisable you have a plan for each prospect.

Have you ever heard the saying, "If the only tool you have is a hammer, you tend to see every problem as a nail"? Your customers are not all nails. You cannot use the same tool to fix everything. Prospecting is no different. For example, you are not going to reach the C-suite using the same process you would to reach an individual lower in the organization.

You must segment your prospects by the type of message and strategy that will most likely engage them. An individual lower in the organization is more likely to take a phone call than someone in the C-suite who is not going to talk to anyone they do not know and trust.

Your efforts must also have different timelines associated with them. Your prospecting timelines and the frequency of your efforts are going to vary based on who you are trying to reach. For example, if you are selling into academia, trying to reach a professor at the start of the academic year is simply not going to work. Conversely, if you are trying to reach a graduate student, the start of the academic year might be perfect. In the corporate world dominated by meetings, calling someone five or ten minutes after the hour is almost guaranteed to result in voicemail. But five to ten minutes before the hour, you have a chance. This is about what works best for your customer; not for you.

You also need to keep in mind the higher up in the organization a person is, the more likely you will run into gatekeepers. You need to have a plan for when a gatekeeper answers your call rather than your target. And the more likely you will be able to reach your target and avoid the gatekeeper by using contacts with whom they are already comfortable with. Think referrals (more to come on this in a later chapter).

"You must plan to win, prepare to win, and expect to win." - Zig Ziglar

It is time to wrap up the chapter focused on prospecting success. To help do so what follows is Anthony Iannarino's perspective on the matter of tailoring your messaging:

"Not all clients are created equal. Neither are all prospects. It's easy to spend your time with prospects who are receptive, who are willing to meet with you. But the real results you need in sales only come from pursuing your 'dream clients,' those prospects for whom you can create breath-taking, jaw-dropping, earth-shattering value.

Your 'dream clients' allow you to build real, sustainable results. You will never win these clients if you don't start spending time working on them now. They aren't easy to win, and it takes time. But it's what produces outsized results."

That says it all and is why it is so important to build your prospecting process around gaining information. The best way to do this is by asking questions or posing scenarios designed to allow the customer to share their true needs.

You then combine your questions and the information obtained from asking them with your review of why customers have bought from you in the past, to build out options you can use going forward that best benefit your customers. It is that easy.

As this chapter comes to a close, please remember that reading something is great, but unless you take the next step to put your learning into action, the content will fade away. Again, I offer my reading rule to help you do this. It is that at a minimum I must take one thing, one lesson learned, one key takeaway, one something from what I read - and implement it into my daily life.

Given this and based on the content we just covered in this series, I am going to help you accomplish this. It is simple. All you need to do is complete these follow-up activities:

– Successful Positivity Follow-Up Activities –

- Take the time to answer each of the seven strategic questions regarding your prospecting process. Write down or type out your answers and be candid.

- Take the time to answer each of the thirty tactical questions to measure your effectiveness and process. Write down or type out your answers and be candid.

- Take the time to answer each of the seven questions to build your prospecting plan. Write down or type out your answers and be candid.

"Powerful words come with powerful intent. Where you have passion, strength, courage, and determination you can accomplish anything." - K.L. Toth

Chapter Seven

– How to...Infinite Positivity –

It is a new day full of possibilities. How are you going to choose to spend it? What are you going to do today?

Prospecting is not something you do when you do not have anything else to do. It is not something you do when you suddenly find yourself without enough business, opportunities, or customers. Prospecting is something you must do routinely.

I do the same thing every morning and have for years. I get up early, drink a giant glass of water, then read a chapter of a book. Prospecting should be routine like that. If it is not currently, you now know what you must do today - create your prospecting routine.

If you are not one for routines, fine; if it helps, view prospecting the same way you do taking a shower. I assume you take a shower daily, right? You should prospect daily as failing to do so on a routine basis puts you in a situation where your sales will constantly come in peaks and valleys, which is not a good thing.

You must plan for prospecting time in your schedule otherwise it will not get done. And this does not mean just adding it to your list of things you want to get done. You must actually block the time on your calendar. I will walk you through how to do this and how to create your prospecting routine.

Step 1 – Actually do it. Thinking about prospecting and preparing to prospect are not the same as prospecting. You cannot block an hour on your calendar to only spend that time preparing to prospect. When you block time, include time for preparation. This may mean setting aside twice as much time as you think you will need.

Step 2 – I am a very analytical person. When setting up my calendar it helps me to divide it into parts. For example, if you work a 40-hour week, you have four 10-hour periods to work with, or five 8-hour periods to work with – however you want to slice and dice it. The point is you need to block your time. Do so based on what works best for you and your customers. Here is a simple model you can try:

- 25% (10-hours) Prospecting – Developing leads and qualifying prospects

- 25% (10-hours) Existing Accounts – Connecting with your existing customers

- 25% (10-hours) Sales Calls/Proposals – Making calls on prospects in the middle of the sales funnel, the high-potential prospects, and customers with whom you are trying to close more deals

- 25% (10-hours) Customer Follow-Up/Admin – Taking care of customer issues, attending sales meetings, and completing administrative work

You cannot tell me you do not need or cannot spare time to dedicate 25% of your time to prospecting. If anything that percentage should be higher as prospecting is what keeps your sales engine running.

"To bring one's self to a frame of mind and to the proper energy to accomplish things that require plain hard work continuously is the one big battle that everyone has. When this battle is won for all time, then everything is easy." - Thomas A. Buckner

Step 3 – Remember this is not about you. It is about your customers. Make sure the time you block best aligns with your prospect's time and when you can actually reach them as that is the point of all of this. We covered this earlier in the book, but ask yourself the following questions when you block time for actual prospecting:

- Is it a time when the person I am trying to reach is most likely available?

- Is it a time when you are mentally prepared to engage the person you are trying to reach?

Sometimes these two periods conflict with each other. Your challenge is to find a way to align these times so you can answer "yes" to both questions in order to maximize your success.

Step 4 – Don't start what you cannot finish. It cannot be emphasized enough - prospecting is not about the initial outreach. You are not looking for "one and done" or "spraying and praying" here. You are looking for consistency. Do not make the mistake of thinking you are being efficient by making a bunch of calls or sending a bunch of e-mails once. The goal of prospecting is to create awareness with those who might do business with you and to add value, so they choose to engage with you. You cannot accomplish this with a single phone call or e-mail. Before you start your prospecting, ask yourself if you have the time and ability to make the necessary follow-ups with the people you want to reach. Answering this question truthfully can and will save you a tremendous amount of time.

"Time is the most valuable coin in your life. You and you alone will determine how that coin will be spent. Be careful that you do not let other people spend it for you." - Carl Sandburg

Prospecting is not about going after whoever will talk with you or whomever you get routed to the first time you break through to the company you are trying to reach. If it were, you could just call your mom. I am sure she would love to hear from you and would be more than happy to take your call. That does not make her a prospect though. Prospecting is about focusing your efforts on the person(s) with the greatest potential to allow you to earn the business.

Remember buyers who buy based on tactical reasons tend to be economic buyers, while buyers who buy based on strategic needs are solution buyers. Solution buyers provide you with a better opportunity to help them as they are looking for a solution that usually comes with a long-term partnership, not just a single transaction here and now.

What does this mean to you in your prospecting process? It means a lot. You need to determine early on why the prospect is willing to talk with you. What is their need? How can you help them with it? If the prospect is not willing to share their business needs with you, then you are probably not talking to the right person.

Do not think just because you are talking to the "user" or "owner" of what you are selling that they will see the value you can offer. Some "users" are so close to the way they have always done things that they may not even know they have a problem or that there could be a better way. Some "owners" may be the ones we developed the current process and have pride in it. These situations probably are not going to lead to the results you want.

"Users" and "owners" can still be a source of valuable information about the current process and about how and who makes decisions in their organization. This information can lead you to the individual who will recognize the strategic benefit of what you are offering. This is where you can help them most and earn the business.

Really though - go call your mom. She misses you and would love to hear about your prospecting plan. She may not understand it, but I am sure she will think it is great. What a fantastic way to infuse some positivity into your day.

"The difference between what we do and what we are capable of doing would suffice to solve most of the world's problems." - Mahatma Gandhi

Have you ever considered visiting the boneyard?

By boneyard, I am referring to your old customers who declined or are no longer doing business with you. Contacting old customers is something new hires should do immediately because they can make the calls without any implication of being "part of the problem" should a customer bring it up. They get the benefit of coming in with a clean slate to ask questions and to understand what may have happened. As the new person, you are free to ask questions a more seasoned employee simply cannot. Do not miss your opportunity to benefit from being the 'new person."

Another great benefit of calling all your old customers is it is a great way to become educated on the company and the industry. During the course of making these calls to old customers, many will share insights with you as the new person.

What a great way for a new salesperson to get educated by making prospecting phone calls to old customers! If you are a sales leader, you should make this part of your onboarding process.

If you are in sales, you should make this part of your 30-60-90-day plan when taking on a new adventure.

What harm would come from a veteran salesperson doing the same?

The answer is none, as they are already a lost customer. A veteran salesperson should absolutely visit the boneyard. A word of caution though - if you were involved with the old customer previously and understand why they are no longer a customer, do not call to ask them why they decided to make a change. You already know. Do not waste theirs or your time. If you are going to call them you should be prepared to share how you addressed whatever gave them a reason to look elsewhere. That will add value and make the call worth it.

"We ought not to look back unless it is to derive useful lessons from past errors, and for the purpose of profiting by dearly bought experience." - George Washington

Before you start your prospecting, you need to complete some basic research. Take note of the word "basic." Your research needs to be only enough to provide you with what you need to make the first contact. That's it. It is literally that simple.

There is no reason to precede every outreach with the type of research you would do if you were drafting a business plan or conducting market research. A quick search on Google or LinkedIn can provide incredible insights, but the important thing to remember is there is no need to get carried away. If that quick search does not provide what you are looking for to initiate contact, check out the news section of the website of the customer you want to connect with. There is always great information you can use there.

Far too many salespeople put off starting their prospecting because they want to do more online research. They want to know everything about the customer and every way they could help them. What if the customer asks a question they cannot answer? They do not want to get caught with their pants down. Isn't it better to invest the time to ensure everything is perfect first?

Remember from an earlier chapter that perfection and procrastination are highly related, and both characteristics are prominently present in salespeople. You can only reach out if everything is perfect! The reality is that it will never be perfect. You will never be able to answer every question that may come up. So, fear will take over and you will never reach out.

Keep in mind that the way to deal with this is to make contact when the information you have is helpful, not when it is perfect. After you have answered the previous questions and you understand your customer, you will know when it is helpful and good enough to make the effort to connect. Until you make the effort to understand your customers the distance between today and perfection is occupied by fear, and it will always prevent you from getting to perfect.

Let that sink in for a minute. It is a good thing you learned how to disarm fear in an earlier post.

Instead of doing a deep dive, use the internet to do three things:

- Identify potential companies and people to prospect
- Identify specific contact information
- Identify a reason for the call

Again, that's it. It is literally that simple. It cannot be stressed enough - the importance of not getting lost in the details when all you really need is one piece of information.

"When you aim for perfection, you find that it's a moving target." - George Fisher

Prospect or not?

This is a question and concept Mark Hunter covers in his book A Mind for Sales. Do you know the difference? You really should!

All too often that person you think is a great prospect is nothing more than someone pretending to be a prospect. Wait! Why would someone pretend to be a prospect? People like attention. They like to feel important and needed. People like to be involved. Think about it. Isn't that exactly what you do as part of your prospecting? Don't you give the prospect your attention by targeting and reaching out to them? Don't you make them feel important and needed by asking them all sorts of questions? Don't you involve them in your work to earn the business? That is kind of a scary thought, right?

Prospects who are not actually prospects do not answer the phone by saying, "hello this is John, and I am really not the best person for you to speak with." Their e-mail signature or LinkedIn profiles do not tell you their level of influence and decision-making abilities. Instead, they hide who and what they are for many reasons.

Sometimes they may be gathering their own information. They may engage with you repeatedly for no other reason than to learn something they can use elsewhere. Others may engage with you because their bosses told them to do so because they (the boss) were too busy. Others engage with you because they do not like to say "no" to others as they do not want to let anyone down or hurt anyone's feelings. My wife fits into this category and it means we get volunteered for a lot of stuff. Some may engage with you because they know the game and if they do so for long enough, they just might get a free meal or some other free benefit.

Think about it. How many times have you spent too much time with someone you thought was a great prospect, only to have them wind up not being who you thought? The longer you have been in sales, the higher this number will be.

Throughout this book, I have conveyed that your time is your most valuable asset as a salesperson. As such, you cannot afford to waste it. On top of that, if you cannot determine if the person you are engaging is the right person, you will never achieve any level of success in sales. The sooner in your process you can validate the intentions of the person with whom you are talking, the sooner you will be using your time efficiently.

Never forget the more time you spend with the wrong people, the less time you will be able to spend with the right ones.

"Pretend that every single person you meet has a sign around his or her neck that says, 'Make me feel important.' Not only will you succeed in sales, you will succeed in life." - Mary Kay Ash

Now that you understand the importance of this question how do you determine who is a prospect and who is not? This should come as no surprise, but I am going to ask you some questions to help guide you to your answer.

Let's start with a BIG one. Do they have a need you can help them with? If not, there is no point in you investing your time into them. Also, if they are not willing to share their need with you, this is another red flag, and you should refocus your time and efforts elsewhere. There are far more important people to whom you can devote your time and effort. People who will help you earn business. Do not put words into the customer's mouth as to how you could help them either. Even if you work with other customers similar to them or if your basic research made you think you could. You can test this by following the rule that unless the customer says it with their own mouth, then you do not believe it. Think about that. Would a person talk about a need if it were not real? No. Make sure they tell you otherwise or move on.

Once they have told you about their need, you then need to understand that need, right? Have they shared with you a piece of proprietary information to help you understand? Again, think about it. Proprietary information is something you would not be able to find any other way unless the person you are talking with shares it. Whether the information is personal in nature or relates to their business is not what is important. What is important is that they shared it. A person is not going to share proprietary information with you unless they have confidence in you and feel there is a reason to do so. Think about it this way - someone who has no intention of buying from you is most likely not going to share something proprietary in nature.

While we are talking about prospecting, it is never too early to understand how the company you are targeting makes decisions. Have they told you when they are going to make a decision? Without understanding this, how are you going to best align your efforts and expectations? If they are not going to decide for months or even years, you need to decide if it is worth investing your valuable time today. There is a big difference between a deal worth $$ and a deal worth $$$$$. Once your time is gone, you cannot get it back. This does not mean you cast them aside never to contact them again. You have to decide if it make sense to work with them and if it does, to then determine when it would make sense to come back together to help them. Then set a reminder to do so. Find and focus your attention on someone who has a need you can help them with today.

"Energy is the essence of life. Every day you decide how you're going to use it by knowing what you want and what it takes to reach that goal, and by maintaining focus." - Oprah Winfrey

Your ability to earn business goes down dramatically if you are dealing with someone who is merely relaying information to the actual decision-maker. How do you make sure your contact is the actual decision-maker? Ask them. Ask them how they have made decisions like this in the past. This question is non-threatening and allows them to share information. As they share you listen for clues as to who will make it and how it will be made.

You can also ask them if there is anyone else who will be involved in making the decision. Again, it is straightforward and designed to ensure you are using both your and their time effectively.

Assuming you have already had them communicate their need with their own mouth, you will also want to understand if others are involved in helping them address their need. In other words, you want to know if a competitor has already shaped their expectations. This could be a request for proposal (RFP) or a quote request you are asked to participate in. The rule I have always used when it comes to this type of business is that you need to be the one to help them create the RFP/quote request. If a competitor helped them create it, why would you think you can earn the business? If you find yourself in this situation, don't walk away, but know you are probably in for an uphill battle.

If you are invited to the discussion at this late stage, not only will it be hard to articulate the value you can bring given the process being used, but you are probably just providing the customer with information they can use to obtain better terms from whoever did help write it. I do not mean to be negative here (Infinite Positivity and all) but being tardy to the party is a kiss of death that in most cases will leave you with nothing to show for your hard work.

Another key question, but one that can be hard to determine, is if they can afford to buy. Who has not wandered through an electronics department of a store without intent to buy? Who has not dreamed of the furniture they would add to their home at a home furnishing store? We've all wasted the time of a salesperson by talking about something we wanted to buy but could not actually buy.

When this happens, the person probably wants to buy but they lack the ability to do so. So, the whole time they come across as being sincere in their intent to buy. A question you can ask to determine their intent is, "When you make big decisions like this, what criteria do you consider?" This question isn't perfect as the customer may still have and articulate a criteria. What should concern you is anything they say that leads you to believe they do not have the money or ability to make the purchase. In these cases, there is value in getting to "no" as quickly as possible and then moving on.

Everyone deserves an opportunity to daydream; you just need to make sure that does not happen on your time.

"The first step towards getting somewhere is to decide you're not going to stay where you are." - John Pierpont "J.P." Morgan

Another way to help validate if the person you are dealing with is a prospect or not, and if they are serious about buying, is to ask them to do something for you.

You would typically make this request at the end of your conversation with them. It also needs to be something realistic; not pie in the sky. You could ask them if they would review and comment on something you send them. You could ask them to send you something pertaining to their need. You could ask them to send you a copy of their confidentiality agreement (CDA/NDA) so they can comfortably send you details about their need.

This is a good gauge of intent as someone who is not interested in moving forward with you will not take the time to do anything extra for you. Doing this does a few things. It allows you to measure their interest. It allows you to move the conversation forward based on what you receive. It gives you a reason for your next conversation with them. And it helps you stay top-of-mind with them after the call.

This is also a good time to make sure you (yes, YOU) are properly keeping track of what you consider as prospects. Prospects = IN. Everyone else = OUT. The last thing you want to do is fill your pipeline with prospects that do not belong there. Doing so does you no good.

What's in your pipeline? Are you stuffing it with leads or prospects that have no chance of ever converting to customers? Are you holding on to them as a way to keep yourself from getting discouraged? Are you keeping them to make yourself look better than your peers? Are you playing games with your numbers?

Thinking you can trick the system to succeed will catch up with you. As such, it is better to get real and treat your pipeline as sacred. It is not a parking lot. You do not have time to play games with it, and you do not have time to use it as an ego builder. Your pipeline is your key to success. It is your key to making your numbers, so treat it as such and use it to your advantage!

"Success isn't always about greatness. It's about consistency. Consistent, hard work gains success. Greatness will come." - Dwayne "The Rock" Johnson

Are you famous? Are you selling something people can't live without?

I assume you are not, but that's okay. You don't have to be. But unless you are somebody famous or you offer a product/service everybody must have, sorry to break the news to you, but your prospects could care less.

What does this mean to you? It means you need to quit making poor phone calls, sending out quick and easy e-mails, or even leaving just plain bad voicemails blathering on about who you are and how amazing your company is.

It is critical you understand your prospects simply do not care! They do not care that you have been in business since 1980. They do not have a collection of suppliers and are missing one from that year. They do not care that you have 55,000 SKUs in your catalog. That sounds complicated. They do not care that your company won an award a couple of years ago. I am sure it is prestigious, but it does not help them in any way whatsoever. I just used a key word - help. That is what they are interested in. How can you help them?

The sooner you can understand this, the sooner you can stop putting just plain poor and lazy outreach attempts into the universe. Far too many salespeople make the mistake of thinking this is all about them and then try to focus their messaging on themselves or their company. If all you are doing is talking about yourself and your company, you are destined for low response rates.

Think about it because you have an opportunity here. If you are suffering from low response rates that means you have to increase your output to achieve your desired outcome - you have to make more calls, send more e-mails, etc. to get the number of responses you want/need. Now think if you improve those response rates. That means you get more responses for less output and that you get to spend more quality time with people you can actually help - you get to make less calls, send less e-mails, etc. Which would you prefer? Which would help you achieve your goals?

As such, let's get into some best practices and even some templates you can modify and use to help you help more people, while achieving better outcomes with less effort.

"You have within you more resources of energy than ever been tapped, more talent than has ever been exploited, more strength than has ever been tested, more to give than you have ever given." - John Gardner

Let's get you your first date!

Now that we have covered what not to do, what should you do?

At the most basic level, you want to make contact with your prospect, preferably by phone, and you want to do two things:

- Find out one piece of information about the company and/or person you are talking to. And,

- Identify and obtain agreement on the next step: either an in-person meeting or another phone call at a designated time.

Think of it like trying to get a first date. You see someone. There is instant attraction. You must meet them and get to know them. What do you do? Do you approach them and tell them you were born in the late-70s and have been growing ever since? Do you approach them and tell them about all the material things you own to see if any of them spark interest? Do you approach them and tell them about that award you won back in middle school? If you do, there are plenty of happy single people and I'm sure you'll be just fine. For the rest of us, you should see the absurdity in this. Then why do you do this in sales when you approach a new customer you believe you can help?

Your first interaction with the customer (or in dating) is not the time to over complicate things. Too many salespeople make the mistake of trying to make a huge information dump immediately for it only to go nowhere. Your first interaction should create a level of confidence and obtain something, anything, to have a second interaction. Keep it simple.

Then during your second interaction you can begin to dig deeper and truly qualify the prospect to ensure they are really a prospect and that you can help them (or date them). Remember the criteria from the previous chapter. Go back and re-read it if you need to.

Attempting to complete all of that on the first interaction is rarely doable, and way too many times if you try to do it all, the end result will be nothing.

Your goal is to quickly capture the other person's attention by helping them see enough value in you that they will share with you information you can use during your next interaction - during your first date.

"Generally speaking, the unhappiest people you will ever meet will be those who are utterly self-absorbed; the happiest people you will ever meet will be those who lose themselves in the joy and challenge of helping others." - Unknown

This sounds great, but what does this look like in real life?

It makes sense that prospects do not care about you, but rather care about how you can help them. It makes sense not to do an information dump on a first interaction, but rather quickly capture attention by helping them see value in you so they share one piece of information you can use during your next interaction. It makes sense to keep the first date simple and to use the second interaction to begin digging deeper to qualify the prospect. But how?

What follows are three ways for you to get a first date. We are going to keep it simple and focus on connecting, providing information, and adding value. That's it.

Connecting is the easiest to use. Simply put, you use a person's name or the industry they are in to catch their attention.

Phone example: "Hello, John, this is Jim with Business123. We helped another (enter company's industry/focus here) company gain production capacity and increased employee safety through a program we developed. Would you have time later this week for a brief call to discuss how we achieved this? I think you'd benefit from it as well."

t does not stop here. You must be prepared to respond however the other person replies. If they say, "no, I don't have time," your response would be either, "when would be a better time for us to discuss how we can help you?" or "are there other more important initiatives you're focused on other than production capacity and employee safety?" Keep in mind your objective with the follow up question is to find out one piece of information you can use when you connect with them at a later time.

Here is an e-mail example of what this could look like:

Subject: Reduced Storage Capacity for (Enter company's industry/focus here)

Sarah,

Storage capacity is a luxury most (enter company's industry/focus here) companies don't have. Addressing this challenge often results in unintended side effects when it comes to availability and consistency of materials. Would reducing the materials you have to store onsite with a guaranteed consistent supply help you accomplish more? We can help you achieve this, like we have with others. Can you please let me know a couple of dates/times next week you will be available for a brief call to discuss how?

Thank you,

Tim Smith

Business123

Notice how it is direct and short. No one has time to read long e-mails. Your objective with the e-mail is not to provide them with so much information that they can immediately make a decision, but rather to help them realize they want to contact you for help.

"Creativity is especially expressed in the ability to make connections, to make associations, to turn things around and express them in a new way." - Tim Hansen

What are the providing information and the adding value approaches when it comes to your initial prospecting outreach efforts?

Let's start with providing information. This approach works great in industries where changes are frequent such as life science with its ever-evolving regulatory landscape, or software where changes are an everyday occurrence. Your goal is to simply convey that you have some critical insights they will find of interest.

Voicemail example: "Hello Bob, this is Jim from Business123, and I have the new ISO regulations that just come out regarding manufacturing and how they affect products like yours. Please call me at 55-55-555 and we can discuss. Again, Jim, 55-55-555."

Using this approach does require that you stay up to date on the latest industry changes to be able to provide value. If you can talk the talk, this approach may be your best option.

What about the adding value approach you ask? This one is all about making a power statement about something then asking for the person's input or for a meeting to discuss it further.

Phone example: "Beth, this is Jim with Business123. There's a real push by many companies to increase revenue generation while reducing costs and mitigating risk. How are you approaching this?"

With this approach, the key is to engage the other person quickly in a conversation and then use what they share as the basis for your next question. Your goal is the same as with the others — to gain a key piece of information you can use as the foundation for your next conversation.

These three simple approaches work if you are using the phone, e-mail, voicemail, social media, or text. Does not matter.

The more you use these techniques, the more comfortable you will be with them, and you will begin to understand better which ones (or variations of them) work best for you.

Do not think for a moment these three techniques are always going to work the first time. Many times, it will take two, three, four, or more contacts before you get any sort of information to move forward (remember the consistency chapter?).

That's why it's so important for you to have and use multiple approaches. Think of your prospect receiving your message. If you were a prospect and a salesperson reached out to you using the same message and approach repeatedly, would you become annoyed with them? Yes. Yes, you would.

The most effective prospectors use multiple approaches and are comfortable alternating between them as situations dictate. If you think you can use one delivery method for your entire prospecting strategy, think again. Also, what you prefer may not be what your prospect prefers.

It's also critical you keep a record of what you're using. This includes the message, the day/time you reached out, and how you reached out. This is where a good CRM system can earn it's keep

"Try not to become a person of success, but rather try to become a person of value." - Albert Einstein

Believe it or not, we've completed another chapter. As such, it's time to ensure what you've read sticks.

Remember the rule - you must take at least one (hopefully more) thing from the reading and implement it into your daily life.

Ashes to ashes. Dust to dust. Implementing just one thing will ensure the time you invested in reading this doesn't fade off into obscurity.

And I will help you. What follows are some follow-up activities that will help you do this.

— How to...Infinite Positivity Follow-Up Activities —

- Complete the four steps associated with the Time-Management Tactics.

- Complete the basic research steps for 10 new prospects. Once completed, repeat for 10 more. Then 10 more. Then 10 more. Keep doing this to fill your funnel.

- Evaluate your top 10 potentials to determine if they deserve to be called prospects. Document your findings and how you got to them.

- Try out the three approaches to get a first date. Keep trying them until you get 10 first dates scheduled. Once completed, repeat. Continue doing so and then start scheduling second dates.

"An organization's ability to learn, and translate that learning into action rapidly, is the ultimate competitive advantage." - Jack Welch

Chapter Eight

— Infinite Positivity in Reality —

A reminder and an example...

We are making great progress with the Infinite Positivity sales model, but before we continue any further, we are going to take a break to focus our attention on a real-life example of Infinite Positivity to illustrate how you could help your customers solve challenges they faced and in doing so transformed your relationship with them from a transactional one, to a strategic partnership.

What follows is a case study demonstrating what you should strive to achieve with your customers as once you help them solve a challenge, who do you think they will call next time they find themself faced with a new challenge?

Case Study:

How we prevented an inevitable disruption to manufacturing and helped ensure the gift of tissue donation using a combination of our catalog products and custom manufacturing capabilities.

Background:

The customer, a tissue processor, a company that manufactures tissue grafts and biologics from donated human musculoskeletal tissues, was utilizing a gentamicin sulfate solution, an antibiotic that inhibits the growth of a wide variety of Gram-positive and Gram-negative microorganisms, as part of their aseptic manufacturing process.

Challenge:

The gentamicin sulfate solution they had qualified for their process was manufactured as a drug for patient applications. The manufacturer of this drug found themselves in a situation in which patient demand was outpacing their manufacturing which resulted in the gentamicin sulfate solution being put on allocation. The customer was not using the gentamicin sulfate solution to treat patients, but rather for further manufacturing, so they were placed at the bottom of the allocation list for receiving more solution. The customer was fortunate to maintain a safety stock of the solution; however, the allocation had depleted their safety stock putting them in a situation in which they only had enough solution to support processing for 2-3 weeks. Due to the nature of the tissues the customer works with, not processing or delaying their processing was not an option as doing so would put the gift of the donated tissue in jeopardy.

"No one who achieves success does so without the help of others. The wise and confident acknowledge this help with gratitude." - Alfred North Whitehead

Solution:

After understanding the customers' situation and their specific needs for the gentamicin sulfate solution, two solutions were developed and proposed.

The first was a short-term solution to address their immediate need and to prevent any disruption to their ability to process. This solution entailed providing them with the gentamicin sulfate antibiotic in powdered form, as well as with bottles of USP Sterile Water for Injection, so they could manufacture the gentamicin sulfate solution themselves in their cleanroom at the time of use. Given chemical and reagent manufacturing was not one of their core capabilities, a manufacturing procedure they could follow was compiled and provided to them.

The second was a long-term solution and it was designed to provide them with a like-for-like solution to what they were purchasing and using, the one difference being what we provided would not be a drug, which was not a requirement of theirs. They had simply used the drug version as that was what was readily available when they established their process. This solution entailed us custom manufacturing the gentamicin sulfate solution for them so that upon receipt they would have a ready-to-use version of the solution they had been using. The same formulation was used. The same preservatives and additives were added. The same specifications were tested and met. The same fill volume was used. It was equivalent in every way that mattered to them.

The reason for the two solutions was to provide a short-term antimicrobial reagent for the customer to continue operations while the second long-term solution was being validated. Only proceeding with the custom ready-to-use option would have meant the customer depleted their safety stock and their processing would have been adversely impacted. Instead, we were able to address their immediate needs as well as create a more sustainable supply to best support their future needs. Both of which ensured their ability to process their tissues in order to continue to provide the world with their lifesaving and life-enhancing tissue grafts.

That is Infinite Positivity in action!

Who do you think they will call next time they have a need after this?

"Never look down on someone unless you're helping them up." - Jesse Jackson

Chapter Nine

– Infinite Positivity via Phone and/or Voicemail –

There is no reason with all of the information available today for anyone to have to make a cold call.

If you are making cold calls, you are simply being lazy.

Remember the basic research approach from the previous chapter? Given the massive amount of information available to you I suggest the term cold calling is officially retired and informed calling used instead.

Informed Calling is a significantly better approach as it is informed because the call you are making has a reason based on your basic research and how you can help the person on the other end. As we have covered, the reason is to gain information, because you know you can help based on something you have already learned about them. Do not complicate things. This information can and should be basic. It could be limited to knowing they are in the same industry as other customers you work with. Because you are calling to help them, when you are making informed calls, you are providing a service to the person you are calling.

Keep in mind most salespeople spend little time on the phone, but this mode of communication allows you to gather information and establish/build your relationship in real-time. E-mails, text, social media do not offer this.

Before you start making excuses as to why you do not use the phone more, let me stop you as I have heard them all.

I can't tell you how many salespeople have told me how hard it is to find phone numbers. Really?

There are plenty of ways to find phone numbers and it all starts with saying, "I'm not going to let an obstacle stand in my way."

Also, if a phone number is hard for you to get, it also means it's hard for your competition to get. That combined with the fact that your competition is not spending much time on the phone can be a huge differentiation for you. Think about it – a call from an enthusiastic salesperson intent on helping whoever you are calling, or a cold lazy e-mail that may end up unread in a junk folder? The choice is pretty simple.

"Work joyfully and peacefully knowing the right thoughts and right efforts inevitably bring the right results." - James Allen

If you are still of the mind that it's too hard to find phone numbers, I am going to help you by sharing some easy ways for you to find the number you are looking for:

- Check the company's website for the person you are trying to reach. Even if this gets you to a dial-by-name directory or an operator you can work with that.

- Search the person's profile on LinkedIn. There is a section for contact information.

- Find someone you know that also knows the person you are trying to reach and ask them for a phone number. Or better yet, an introduction.

- Utilize a program such as ZoomInfo, which for a small charge you can get access to a lot of contact information.

- Reach out to the Chamber of Commerce in the city where the company is located. Again, even if this gets you to a dial-by-name directory or an operator that is a win.

- Use Twitter to find the company's handle and any contact information or check Facebook to find a company's business page.

- Contact an industry trade association they are likely to be associated with. Often times companies have to register using their contact information with these associations.

- Contact someone you know at a supplier you know the company you're trying to reach uses. Again, this is an opportunity to ask for an introduction.

- This one should probably be first on the list but search your CRM system and files.

Are some of these not part of your typical approach? Good. That is the point. Get creative and remember (say it with me) - "I'm not going to let an obstacle stand in my way."

Anyone who says they cannot find a phone number is simply putting in any effort and this is the easiest excuse salespeople make as to why they do not use the telephone for prospecting. Now that you have read this, you are not allowed to use this excuse. Put in the work. You can do it!

Searching for phone numbers can also help with your basic research as it may help you uncover valuable information you can use on your first date (call). This is why there is no reason to ever have to make a cold call. Instead, choose to make informed calls.

"Let's dream big but realize that hard work, resilience, discipline, staying-focused and making short-term sacrifices are the critical components for success." - Tony O. Elumelu

If you believe calling someone out of the blue is rude, ask yourself - do you offer them something beneficial?

Of course, you do! That's why you do what you do!

Do not allow yourself to believe every call you make is going to reach the other person at a perfect time. You will be rejected and ignored.

The phone game is all about persistence. You must be persistent, as tenacity will ultimately win. You may not reach the prospect today, tomorrow, or even next week. It may take months or even a year, but you will succeed.

How do I know you will succeed? Simple. You will succeed because you...

- Make the call about the person you are calling, not about you. The reason for the call must be to provide information or insight they find a value. You should have three questions ready you can ask them and/or three benefit statements they will find valuable.

- Speak with energy and believe in yourself. If you do not believe in yourself and speak with confidence and energy, why should you expect the person you are calling to pay any attention?

- If a door closes on you, you find a different door. Do not think for a second, there is only one phone number (or person) you can call.

 Be prepared, regardless of who answers the call. Odds are you go one of three ways – the person you are trying to reach answers, a gatekeeper answers, or your call goes to voicemail. Each requires a different approach from you. Be prepared no matter which way it goes.

- Always use a quality headset to make your calls. We are more effective in our communication when we speak with our hands, even when the other person can't see us. Get up and move around. It will help.

- Use the day wisely and keep records of when you call and what you say. Many people are easiest to reach before eight in the morning or after five in the evening. Experiment with different times to learn what times works best for the person you are trying to reach; it will differ person to person.

- Do not think you will make one call and be done. Be prepared to call the same person a number of times to finally be able to break through. A strategy to use is six contacts in a month, maximum. If after a month you're not successful, then back off for a month or two and then repeat the process.

- Do not leave the same voicemail twice with the same person. Don't be lazy. Leaving the same message repeatedly is a quick way for the person you're trying to reach will lose respect for you. Also remember you will increase your odds of reaching the person by calling them on different days and different times.

- Calling right before the top of the hour to reach busy people. Most meetings start at the top of the hour, which means the one time you might be able to catch the person is after one meeting ends and the next one starts.

- Never give up. It's easy to think the telephone isn't effective and that using e-mail or even social media is the better way to go. The only reason people think that is because they are not willing to put in the effort and time to make telephone prospecting a part of their overall prospecting plan. But you are different.

You make it happen!

"Always believe in yourself and keep going. You don't have to have the most talent in the world. You don't have to be the smartest person in the world. If you persist and you persist and you persist, you will be successful." - Dean Cain

Prospecting using the phone is a key differentiator for you as again, most salespeople would rather send an e-mail and think they accomplished something. That isn't you though. You live the Infinite Positivity model, you have things you want to accomplish, and you know the best opportunity to accomplish those things is via a live conversation. Unless you are a road warrior with an unlimited travel budget, that leaves you with the phone.

To clarify the term phone has evolved in recent years. Pre-pandemic, it literally only meant making calls from a landline or a mobile. Today, post-pandemic, this term is now more common to be a video call via Microsoft Teams or Zoom. What we are talking about can be used for either plain old voice calls, or the more modern video calls. Video calls give you the best of both worlds as you get to see and react to a person live as you have the conversation. It is the closest thing you can do to actually being in the room with the person, but without the travel costs and time.

So, you make your initial informed call, as we have been discussing, and you get through. What next? What do you do to get the conversation started? Do not worry, I am going to help you by providing some simple ways to start your call – conversation starters.

The goal with each of the examples I will share is to allow you to get a conversation going. Remember - you have two objectives you are trying to accomplish with your initial call. You want to make the person you are calling feel comfortable with you, so you can gain one piece of information from them you can use at a later date to advance the conversation. Then, with the insight you learn, you want to establish a time for your next interaction.

The best way to respect your prospect's time is to share key information that allows them to quickly understand you care about their business and can help them.

While you have been planning for this call with your basic research, please keep in mind that they are most likely not planning to hear from you. They have other things on their plate to accomplish. On top of that, you are not the only salesperson reaching out to them. This is why it is critical to focus on adding value by helping them with something on their plate, while being respectful of their time.

To best do this, you should open the conversation with something meaningful that will resonate with them, as well as lead to discovering more information from them. Doing so will ensure you end up with a conversation that benefits you both.

"It takes a special mind to formulate the relevant questions and ask them at the right time." - Sam Dey

Here are some conversation starter templates to get you going:

- Hello, I'm _____ with _____. Are you the person in charge of buying _____? How have you been dealing with _____? How interested would you be in _____?

- Hello, is this _____? I'm _____ with _____. After supporting other customers in the _____ like yourself, our customers have been able to _____ by working with us. What would those types of results look like for you?

- Hello, I'm _____ with _____. We have _____ that works with _____ which you're already using. Who is your current supplier? How are they doing for you? Can you tell me more?

- Hello _____. Thank you for taking my call. I'm _____ with _____. There are new studies out regarding _____. This looks like it will create significant _____ in less time than before. Where does something like this fit into your business plan?

- Hello _____. I'm _____ with _____. We have been working with _____ industry and have seen major _____, which from what I've been told is something you're working on, too. How is the project going for you?

- Hello _____. I'm _____ with _____. I just saw where you announced _____. We just got done helping another company do the same thing. What are the goals you're looking to achieve from this?

- Hello, is this _____? My name is _____ with _____. What have been the results you've been able to see from _____? I've heard the same thing from others and that's why _____. What would your business look like if you were to _____?

- Hello, I'm _____ with _____. We help others like you achieve _____. Have you been able to _____ in the last year? How do you intend to handle _____ in the future?

Hello, I'm _____ with _____. Your company has been able to achieve significant progress doing _____. What do you feel has been the reason for your success? We have some items that would allow you to _____, resulting in _____. How important would something like that be to you?

Notice none of these blather on about who you are or how amazing your company is. They are straightforward, to the point, about sparking quick interest, while adding value, and to engage the customer in something relevant to them you can help them with.

"My first rule of a conversation is this: I never learn a thing while I'm talking. I realize every morning that nothing I say today will teach me anything, so if I'm going to learn a lot today, I'll have to do it by listening." - Larry King

Does anyone actually listen to voicemails anymore?

I have two teenage kids. The phone app on their phones is probably the least used app. They simply do not make phone calls unless that is the only option, or their annoying dad calls them. I am pretty sure both of them have intentionally not set up their voicemail boxes. I am pretty sure they would lose their minds if I or anyone else left them a voicemail. There is definitely no way they are checking it and returning the call.

Okay, but that is kids. What about adults? What about the people you are wanting to reach so you can help them? Adults are different, right?

I am not sure they are. Leaving voicemails can work when used properly, and assuming your expectations are reasonable. You should treat voicemails as a tool in your prospecting toolbox. As is the case with each tool, it has unique advantages over the other tools. Certain tools will resonate better with certain people as compared to other tools as well.

Voicemails can be a way for you to demonstrate your confidence and energy to the person you are attempting to reach. You can show your respect for their time by leaving a short and concise message. Voicemails can help build awareness and serve as a form of advertising, helping the person you are calling to become more familiar with you. You can also demonstrate your hard work and persistence by leaving messages at different times of the day. Best of all, voicemails allow the person you are calling to listen to the messages at their convenience.

On the other hand, leaving a good message takes time to learn and practice. Voicemails can also be a little harder to track in your CRM system. And you need to be honest with yourself that there is a chance the person you are calling will not listen to the message; however, this possible outcome is no greater than with any other prospecting tool you might use.

As such, voicemails are not a slam dunk, guaranteed to get you a call back. But they only take a minute to leave and assuming you leave a clear, concise message, you really don't have anything to lose.

"Do not wait: the time will never be 'just right.' Start where you stand, and work with whatever tools you may have at your command and better tools will be found as you go along." - Napoleon Hill

Given the question of whether or not your message will be listened to, or better yet your call returned, your goal should be to make your voicemail as effective as possible. So how do you accomplish this and increase the odds of your call being returned?

One of the biggest mistake people make is leaving a message with zero value to the person receiving it. As we have already covered, the person you are calling doesn't care about you and they certainly don't want to hear how wonderful you are blather about what you and your company do. Leave a message like this and you can almost guarantee it will be deleted after just a few seconds.

Think about it this way - did the person you are calling wake up this morning, jump out of bed, race to their calendar where they have "receive a call from a random person" circled? Do you think they are going to start their day and just sit there waiting and hoping you will call them?

No, they have things to do, probably a lot of things to do, many of which are important to them. You must understand this, and you must keep this in mind when you decide on what to say in your message. Your message must contain a value statement that benefits the person you are calling. You need to make it about them and what is important to them. Voicemail is also not the place for any fluff. This means you need to summarize one piece of information they will find a value in a single sentence.

That is your prep work before making any call. What is your one-line value add that is relevant for this specific person you are calling? If you don't have it, you are not ready to make the call. Proceeding with the call without your one-line value add is most likely going to result in a long, meaningless message that never gets returned. It's your choice.

As we did with the conversation starters, I am going to help you with some of these one-line value adds.

"The greatest gift is the power to estimate correctly the value of things." - Le Rochefoucauld

As we continue to address the modern question of whether or not people still listen to voicemail, I have a question for you.

That phone you have in your pocket, your purse, on your desk, or in your hand right now. I want you to envision a scenario in which it rings. Caller ID shows an unknown number, so you send the call to voicemail. Shortly thereafter you get a notification that you have a voicemail. So, you play the message, and you hear the following:

"Hello, I'm calling looking for the person who is in charge of new customers. My name is Jim, and I'm with Business123. We specialize in helping companies like yours accomplish amazing things. We've been in business for more than 20 years and over that time have won numerous awards, which means the systems and methods we use really work. Each time we work with a company, we are able to help them become more successful. What is even better is we have plans to fit all sizes of companies and budgets. Each plan has a variety of different support services such as cost saving models, sourcing redundancy, improved speed to market, operational efficacy, and anything else you need. We don't require long-term contracts and we found most of our customers like our 30-day plans. We can also work with you on payment terms depending on your business and the project. If you aren't the person responsible for this, please have the person who is call me back at 55-55-555, extension 5 and ask for me, Jim."

So, what do you do? I clocked myself reading this message aloud and it took about a full minute. Did you even make it through the whole message before getting confused or bored? Is this a call you are going to return?

You may be different, but I probably wouldn't listen to the full message, nor would I call Jim back. But why?

This message lacks energy. It is also all about him and his company. It lacks specificity and does not pertain to the person he is trying to reach. Along this same vein, he talks a lot about was how wonderful his company is and the awards they have won. Great for them, but what does that do for me, the recipient? Absolutely nothing; it is not relevant. On top of that, the message is way too long. Did you notice he did not even know who he should be calling? Who would be willing to forward a voicemail like that? Then at the end, he ended the call by giving a phone number and extension only once. Even if I wanted to call him back, I would have to listen to the message multiple times to understand the number because it was only left once.

So, this message is not how you set yourself up best to have your call returned. Hopefully, we can agree on that. What do you do then?

"To add value to others, one must first value others." - John Maxwell

Do not expect your call and/or voicemail to be returned. That's right! Your single voicemail is most likely not going to get returned. You may be thinking that is not very positive. No, it is not, but it is true. To turn it into a positive you should leave your message as one of the series of messages you use to reach the person you are trying to reach across different mediums.

As we have covered, your voicemail must contain something of value for the person receiving it. And remember, the message is not about you. That is the last thing they want to hear. Leaving a voicemail with someone who is not looking for you to call them and then blathering on about how great you are is a recipe for a huge disaster. The only thing you will succeed at is stroking your own ego, and along the way you are going to suffer a lack of sales.

Your message must be of interest to the person you are trying to reach. The best way to do this is to look for information they have most likely not seen that you have been able to review. Sharing that you have this type of information in a voicemail can give you critical leverage and it can increase your odds of getting a call back. This is the same approach you would use if they had answered the phone.

The purpose of your voicemail is not to complete a sale. That will come later. The purpose is to engage the person you are trying to reach in a conversation over a period of time. That is why you share information they will value.

The significance of this approach is that most people view salespeople as being clueless about the industry they are selling to, or worse yet, they see salespeople as self-serving. When you leave a voicemail that is not self-serving, but rather focused on the target it also demonstrates you know what you are talking about, you stand apart from the crowd.

"Don't be intimidated by what you don't know. That can be your greatest strength and ensure that you do things differently from everyone else." - Sara Blakely

We have already talked about a lot of this, but it bears repeating. It is that important. I get that you want something more immediately actionable, so that is what we will get into next.

Short Messages = Greater Impact.

Keep your messages short! There are a lot of people who say the key is keeping the message to less than 30 seconds or even 20 seconds. Nope. Even that is still way too long! Remember people are busy with a million and a half things on their plate. You probably aren't going to get 20-30 seconds until you demonstrate you deserve it. Keep your voicemail short; 12 second to 18 seconds. Yes, getting a message down to 12 to 18 seconds is tough, but it can be done. You just have to be strategic and intentional with what you choose to say.

Go over 12-18 seconds and you are setting yourself up for one outcome, as only one thing happens to a lengthy message - it gets deleted. Even worse than being deleted is having a prospect remember it was you who left the lengthy message when you are eventually able to connect with them.

Brevity with voicemail is key. You must be concise with no wasted words, such as including your title.

So, what makes a good voicemail message?

Three simple things. That is all you need. You need...

- A concise open – "Seth this is John Smith with Business123."

- A one-line value add – "I have new information regarding changes to the FDA regulations. I would be happy to share this with you."

- A means for them to get back to you – "Please give me a call back at 55-55-555 and we can discuss. Again, Seth this is John, 55-55-555."

t is also important that you do not forget what you said in the voicemail. As such, be sure to keep detailed notes in your CRM system, because think what happens when Seth calls you back to learn about the FDA changes. The last thing you want to do is have your call returned and you not remember the value you offered.

The idea with this simple technique is not to detail what you do and how great your company is in the value statement you leave in the message. The object is to share one sentence that lets them know you have something of value that could help them.

As mentioned previously, your single voicemail is probably not going to get returned. This means you may end up leaving multiple messages for the same person throughout your efforts to get in contact with them. Using voicemail as part of your prospecting campaign is not a license to leave the same message twice with the same person. This is an insult because you need to always assume the person heard the first message and chose not to respond. Think about it - how would you feel if a salesperson left you a duplicate message? Would you take the time to call them back, or would you think them lazy and unimaginative?

"Small things done consistently in strategic places create major impact." - Unknown

Let's bring it all together now as we have covered a lot when it comes to leaving a voicemail that stands a chance of getting listened to and your call returned.

Simplicity is best. That is why you are only going to include three things: a concise open, a one-line value add, and a means for them to get back to you. You are also going to keep your voicemail to 12-18 seconds in length. You will know it fits this time limit as you will practice it beforehand so you have it ready to go should your call not get answered. This is Infinite Positivity where you leave the person you are contacting and their situation better as a result of your involvement, so you are going to provide information they will value and want to receive. You are going to be clear and confident with your message. Stand up, focus, and be intentional with your words. You are going to include your phone number twice and say it slowly, enunciating each digit.

You are not going to include any fluff and you are certainly not going to mention your website address or say when you are available. If your website provides the person you are attempting to contact with the same information you intend to, and they do not have to call you back to get the information – forget it; you are never getting a call back then. The same thing goes for asking them to call you back at a certain time. I get it, I like to plan out my schedule as well, but it is your job to be available for them; not their job to be available for you.

You are going to use EarPods to free you up to be able to speak with your hands. You are going to meticulously notate in your CRM what message you left to ensure you never leave the same message twice and to prepare should they call you back. You are going to leave your subsequent messages on different days of the week at different times of the day. Consider recurring weekly meetings. If someone is busy Tuesday at two in the afternoon one week, there is a good chance they will be busy the following Tuesday at two as well. Your creative! You rotate your call days and call times.

You understand the power of using the very favorite word of the person you are calling. Before you start stressing that you do not know anyone's favorite word, think about it as you do. It is their name. People love to hear their name. That is why when you go into Starbucks to order your favorite drink you are asked your name. That is why they write it on your cup and why they shout it when your drink is ready. Sure, this helps the baristas keep track of the orders (numbers would accomplish this as well), but this is all about creating a positive experience. Knowing this, you use the person's first name twice in your message. No need to waste valuable time saying their last name though; business today is not that formal. But...if you are talking to a doctor or someone with a PhD you may want to forgo their first name in favor or a more formal approach as they often like to hear the respect.

"You cannot hope to make progress in areas where you have taken no action." - Epictetus

And, if all of that isn't enough, you use voicemail along with other outreach methods, as you know that some people simply do not check their voicemails and the last thing you want to do is leave someone message after message, and nothing ever happens. You are smart though and you make sure your prospecting strategy includes multiple outreach methods.

That is another chapter down and now it is time to ensure what you have read sticks. It is time to take at least one (hopefully more) thing from the reading and implement it into your daily life to ensure the time you invested in reading this doesn't fade away.

And as with previous chapters, I am going to help you. What follows are some follow-up activities that will help you do this.

— Infinite Positivity via Phone and/or Voicemail Follow-Up Activities —

- Reread the different ways to get a phone number portion of this chapter and add other ways you use to get phone numbers.

- Reread the portion of this chapter that covers how prospecting using the phone is a key differentiator.

- Reread the conversation starters to get you going and write five more of your own design.

Reread the portion of this chapter covering how to leave a voicemail that stands a chance of getting listened to and your call returned. Then write five messages you could leave and practice each one at least five times. Don't forget to time yourself.

"In both our actions and our thinking habits, tenacity is often the difference between success and failure, fulfillment and frustration." - Philip Dow

Chapter Ten

– More Infinite Positivity in Reality –

Another reminder and example...

We are making great progress with the Infinite Positivity sales model, but before continuing, we are again going to stop, take a break, and focus on a real-life example of Infinite Positivity to show how you can help your customers solve their challenges and in doing so transformed your relationship from a transactional one, to a strategic partnership.

What follows is another case study demonstrating what you should strive to achieve with your customers as once you help them solve a challenge, who do you think they will call next time they find themself faced with a new one?

Case Study:

How we built supply chain redundancy using a global supply chain to provide a specialized reagent (Ficin) when none could be found.

Background:

The customer, a medical device manufacturer focused on soft tissue reconstruction, was purchasing Ficin and using it as a standard reagent in their process as an off-the-shelf product from a well-known life science catalog company. They were experiencing supply chain issues that were severely impacting their production schedule.

Challenge:

In addition to not being able to get their hands on the Ficin, when they did get it, they could only buy this material in bulk. This meant they had to repackage the material themselves to the 47.6g units used in their product. Also, as part of their internal QC process the customer did their own testing on each lot of Ficin they received since their supplier didn't perform this testing.

Solution:

As a global company with manufacturing capabilities on every continent, we were able to use an established relationship with a supplier in Europe that made quality Ficin that met the customer specifications. We ordered three lots of material for them to test via their validation method. They did their internal testing and the material passed for all three lots.

We also set up a process to provide them ready-to-use units prepackaged to 47.6g rather than providing them a bulk unit to eliminate the issuance (weighing) portion of their process and in order to allow them to reallocate those resources to other more important activities.

We also ensured we found a way to include the internal quality control testing and that the results of that testing would be included on the Certificate of Analysis (COA) we provided with every lot. We did this so the customer could forgo performing this testing internally and again reallocate their resources to more important activities.

The customer decided to proceed, and we became their supplier for Ficin. In doing so we were able to provide them with redundancy to their supply chain, provide them a ready-to-use product, allow them to reallocate a good amount of their resources to other areas of their business, as well as help them to attain the material they needed to support their manufacturing.

That is Infinite Positivity in action!

"Words can inspire, thoughts can provoke, but only action truly brings you closer to your dreams." - Brad Sugars

Chapter Eleven

– Infinite Positivity via E-mail –

Stop!

Before you send one more prospecting e-mail, you need to stop and take the time to develop an overall strategy and plan for how to proceed. The easiest approach is to split your contact frequency between phone calls and e-mail: one-half phone calls and one-half e-mails. If you're in an industry where social media is prevalent, then you can go one-third on each: e-mail, telephone, and social media. Regardless, you need a plan.

Sending e-mails by themselves is a complete waste of time. Worse yet, you could wind up getting your e-mail address pegged as spam, destined for a junk folder never to see the light of day. How is that going to help you achieve your goals? The content you use in an e-mail is content you can use in a phone call; just remember not to mirror it. The last thing you want to be seen as is a lazy salesperson who sends the same information using different methods. But we are talking about leaving the person you are contacting and their situation better as a result of your involvement, so you already understand that.

Before you say it, I am going to stop you. Finding e-mails is not hard. It is actually much easier than finding a phone number and since you mastered that in the last chapter this should be a piece of cake. So how do you find an e-mail address?

Simple. Once you identify who you want to e-mail, assuming you don't have their e-mail address, you first go to their website. Once there you go to the contact us page. At a bare minimum you will find the end of the e-mail address, the @company.com portion. In some cases, you will find an actual person's e-mail address that you can use to mimic for the person you identified. From here if you still don't have the e-mail address you need, go to the press releases or news portion of their website. Open a few of their recent press releases and scroll to the bottom. Often times you will find an actual person's e-mail address that again you can mimic for the person you identified. Still don't have what you are looking for? Then it is time to go fishing.

"I think all people naturally desire for things to come to them quickly and easily, including personal growth. The secret isn't really to want more or want it faster. It's to put more time and attention into what you have and what you can do now. Give three times the effort and energy to grow yourself. And allow yourself to grow slowly and with deep roots. Remember that a squash vine or tomato plant grows in a matter of weeks, produces for several days or weeks,

and then dies when the first frost comes. In comparison, a tree grows slowly – over years, decades, or even centuries; it produces fruit for decades; and if health, it stands up to frost, storm, or drought." - John C. Maxwell

Let's go fishing! Fishing for e-mail addresses.

Most e-mails follow a standard format. The most commonly used format is the first initial of the first name combined with last name. You already know the @company.com portion from visiting their website, so you are good to go.

Read further to learn about the e-mail subject and content, but once you understand all of that, try it. There are two outcomes – your e-mail goes through, or it gets bounced as undeliverable. If the former, you are in! If the latter, it is time to try again.

This time open two e-mails. In one use the full first name of the person you identified and then either a dot (.) or an underscore (_) followed by their last name at the @company you already know. As an example, say we are wanting to contact Dean Smith – you would use dean.smith@company.com and dean_smith@company.com. Then you send and wait.

Same two outcomes as before with a slight difference. One e-mail goes through, you are in, either way. Both e-mails bounce, you try again.

At this point you will have covered the vast majority of e-mail formats, but some companies can be tricky. From here there are a few more options you can try. Sticking with our Dean Smith example, these options are as follows:

- Dean@company.com

- Dean.s@company.com

- d.smith@company.com

- smith@company.com

If all of these get returned, check the .com portion. Is the contact/company you are trying to contact in a different country? Maybe you need to change the end of the e-mail address and repeat this process. For example, if your contact is in Canada they may have .ca at the end of their e-mail address. Try it. You have nothing to lose.

As a quick note academic e-mail addresses can be some of the most challenging as a good deal of them include some numerical portion that you will never be able to guess. Think about how many people with the name of Dean Smith may attend a university. They have to differentiate them somehow.

After all these attempts you are still getting a bounced undeliverable response, you can stop. Stop attempting via e-mail. At this point you want to shift your focus from e-mail to either phone or social media. We already covered phone and we will cover social media in the next chapter, so stay tuned for more.

"Time, effort, and imagination must be summoned constantly to keep a relationship flourishing and growing." - Jim Rohn

Do you consider the e-mails you send to be effective?

Assuming you cracked the code on the e-mail format, prospecting e-mails can be effective if you use them as one, that is right, one, component of your prospecting plan. The key is to keep your e-mails concise and focus on what will interest or benefit the person you are contacting. Your e-mail should be no more than three paragraphs containing two sentences each, as this allows you to convey a single idea without the fluff and garbage prospects don't want to see.

Before you even think about sending another prospecting e-mail, ask yourself these questions:

- Does my e-mail have a call to action? Does it prompt the recipient to do something (like reply)?

- Does it include a one-line value add? We talked about this in chapter nine describing tactics and strategies to use with phone and voicemail. If you are not crystal clear on what a one-line value add is, go back and reread that chapter as this is a critical element of any outreach.

- Does it have a personal connection with the receiver? People work with people, not mindless organizations.

- Is it time sensitive? Why should they devote their time to getting back to you now, rather than later?

These questions are the basic elements of an e-mail. The problem today is too many salespeople, because of their laziness or ineptitude, believed they can simply throw e-mails out like snowflakes. Remember when we talked about spraying and praying?

"You've done it before, and you can do it now. See the positive possibilities. Redirect the substantial energy of your frustration and turn it into positive, effective, unstoppable determination." - Ralph Marston

Salespeople that simply throw e-mails out like snowflakes think if they cover enough people, they will be successful. Ever heard the old saying, even a blind squirrel will find an acorn occasionally? You might get lucky once, but you will never be lucky enough to make your numbers. You have the ability to choose not to be a blind squirrel. Seems a simple choice to me. What about you?

If you've done the homework at the end of each chapter you already have enough information to help you write your content. They will be your guide. Most importantly, do not think merely sending a bunch of e-mails will earn your success. It will not. The best sales prospecting e-mail is upported by a campaign that also includes phone calls and a web/social media presence. This s the big reason most e-mail prospecting campaigns do not work; they are not integrated with other prospecting tools. I am a big believer that if you sent a single e-mail, you should be congratulated on doing nothing. E-mail is one tool of many. Use them all!

Let's get into the actual e-mail. It all starts with the subject line of your e-mail, so what is your subject line doing for you? Is it helping or hurting your odds of receiving a reply?

Think of your subject line like the headline of your e-mail. The same concept that applies to a news headline applies to your e-mail subject line, the objective is to peak interest and get the recipient to read more.

Young Karate Turtle Boys Battle World Ending Plan. Alright, I am interested.

Senate Debates for Days and Arrives at Stalemate. No, thank you.

Extreme, but you get the point. If the subject line doesn't grab your prospects attention, it doesn't matter how good your e-mail is because it won't get read.

"Hard work pays off in the future. Laziness pays off now." - Steven Wright

Let's make sure your e-mail catches the attention of the person you are e-mailing!

Your first challenge is to make sure your subject line (or for that matter, any other part of the e-mail) doesn't contain something spam filters would likely block. If you're looking for a list of words, sorry, but each company has different filters and there isn't a universal list. But you use the Infinite Positivity sales model so do not worry; you have this!

The key is to deliver a subject line that compels the person receiving the e-mail to actually open it. Think about your personal e-mail. Do you open and read every e-mail you receive? No. If your spam filter doesn't help you out, you scan and pick the e-mails to read that you want to. The ones that don't make that cut are quickly deleted. When developing your subject line, putting anything in it about yourself is a kiss of death. It might inflate your ego, but it will do nothing else. Remember this isn't about you.

What works best is to keep the subject line simple. Sounds like a recurring theme - simple! You want your recipient to be interested enough to read the first few words, especially if they are scrolling through their e-mail on their phone, which is how most people read e-mails these days.

Here are some suggestions for what you could include in your subject line:

- The name of an association the person you're e-mailing is involved with. This could also include a conference or meeting you met them at.

- The name of a regulatory agency or government body that has an impact on them. Use big brother to your advantage, just do not be all doom and gloom.

- The name of a person the recipient of the e-mail respects, knows, or trusts. Although, if you have this level of insight, you should be asking from a referral from this well known, respected individual.

- The name of a product or division from another company in their industry or in their community. A competitor or someone they benchmark their success against. Just nothing confidential.

- The date and name of a specific event the person would recognize. You were in Boston at this conference back in May, remember?

The subject line you use must also fit the topic of your e-mail. Bait and switch is not cool and will quickly kill any chance you have of engaging your target. We have all been on the receiving end of e-mails like that. It sucks and it just gets deleted.

"The best way to predict the future is to create it." - Abraham Lincoln

You just landed the perfect e-mail subject, and your target is interested. That is fantastic but does you zero good if it stops there.

The opening sentence of your e-mail should contain words pertaining to increasing revenue generation, reducing costs, and mitigating risk. I debated whether or not to include this, as the last thing I want is for you to sound like any other salesperson. We are doing things differently as we are following the Infinite Positivity sales model. These words can sound like buzzwords, but that is where your one-line value add comes to the rescue and backs you up from sounding like everyone else.

Still, the only way to know for sure which words work best is to try different words. Words and sentences that work well for one industry may not work well in another. Try, evaluate, and learn. That is the key.

So, you have an interesting subject line. Awesome! Love it! Getting a prospect to open your e-mail is only the first step.

Next comes your opening. Your opening sentence must also set the tone and give them a reason to keep reading. This is also where you have to discard all the rules you learned in school about how to write a letter. What you learned in school pertains to the 1800's, not today. Forget it. Taking the first paragraph to introduce yourself and your company and going on to state how much of a privilege it is to be sending the e-mail isn't going to gain you a prospect. I got bored just typing that. Do not be boring. You cannot afford it.

One of the best ways to draft a prospecting e-mail is to think you're writing a tweet or texting someone. Simple. Where have you heard that before?

You have to write succinctly to quickly grab attention. Before digging into specifically what works, let's start with what doesn't. Do not use an opening line or phrase like any of these:

My name is… (you are not Eminem)

I work for… (no one cares)

My company does… (too busy)

We've helped… (still do not care)

We're responsible for… (still too busy)

Want to know what's wrong with these? They are all about you. They scream, look at me! They say, I'm trying to sell you something!

So, you do not have to use these, I want to take a minute to tell you how amazing you are. You work so hard for your customers, and you help them so much with their challenges that you do not need to seek solace in their feedback. You know your value and what you do for everyone. Do not look to them for validation. Doing so makes a horrible first impression and it looks like every other e-mail.

If you learn only one thing regarding e-mailing from this chapter, I hope it is this: prospecting is not about you! It's about them.

"Curiosity is the spark that leads to engagement, innovation, and productivity." - Dr. Diane Hamilton

Now that you know what not to do, what does a great prospecting e-mail look like?

Well, it does not include any graphics or attachments and is only four to six sentences in length, broken into two to three paragraphs. That's it! Four to six sentences. Period.

A prospect e-mail is not the place for 3,000-word detailed analysis of what you can do. This is weird for me to say as I am a super detailed person. I am very analytical, and I want to ensure I cover everything. I have had people I work with tell me notes that go into the CRM should be thorough, not like the works of Henry David Thoreau. Get it? Thorough v. Thoreau? Funny. But, you have to resist the urge. I learned how to – you can too!

To make your e-mail easy to read on a phone, which as mentioned previously is how most people read e-mail these days, be sure to always double-space your paragraphs. You also need to keep your e-mail signature simple. Do not include your company logo or awards you have won. You also don't need to include your e-mail address. Think about that. Why would you type out your e-mail address in your signature so whoever receives your e-mail knows how to reach you via e-mail, when they are already receiving an e-mail from you?

Here is a simple signature line you can use:

Joe Smith
55-55-555
Business123

Now let's bring it all together. Keep in mind the objective of your prospecting e-mail is to create a level of interest to give you the opportunity to have a future discussion with the person you are reaching out to. Based on this objective, here is an example of an ideal prospecting e-mail:

Subject: New FDA Regulations Released

Dear Sara,

FDA has updated regulations regarding laboratory developed tests (LDTs), and companies will have 18 months to comply. The changes are quite extensive, although there are ways to comply without disrupting your business.

We have new information about these changes that we would be happy to share with you as we have been monitoring the situation closely.

Can you please give me a call when your schedule can permit so I can share this information with you, so you too can avoid any compliance issues? Sara, I look forward to talking with you soon.

Thank you,

Joe Smith
55-55-555
Business123

This example is mobile friendly, five sentences, three paragraphs, and all about what will interest the person receiving the e-mail.

Is it going to get a 100% response rate? No, nothing will. But it will get a far higher response than other e-mails you have been using.

"Human beings have an innate inner drive to be autonomous, self-determined, and connected to one another. And when that drive is liberated, people achieve more and live richer lives." - Danie H. Pink

Here are a few more examples:

Subject: Cleanroom Requirement Changes

Dear David,

Beginning this month, new changes for cleanroom requirement have taken effect. Some of the changes are significant and require upgrades to your air handling system.

We have experts that can help you through the process of incorporating these changes with minimal or no impact to your business. Can you please give me a call or reply to this e-mail with a date/time that works best for us to discuss this further?

Thank you,

Joe Smith
55-55-555
Business123

And another:

Subject: Profitable Sales Growth

Dear John,

Discounting to close sales is a major problem for many salespeople. The impact this can have on profitability can be significant. Are you aware of how much the discounts you offer are impacting your business? Some companies are leaving over half a million dollars in potential profit on the table each month.

We have some quick and easy ways to ensure discounting is not used as much and when it is used, it is used in a controlled manner. We would be happy to share these ways with you. Can you please let me know when you could spare a few minutes so we can discuss this further?

Thank you,

Joe Smith
55-55-555
Business123

One more for good measure:

Subject: New Facility Support

Dear Tina,

Getting everything in place for opening a new facility can be a daunting task for many companies. There are new federal guidelines regarding how to establish environmental monitoring within your facility that just came out that I would be happy to walk you through. Given everything else on your plate, we can help make the minor modifications to your monitoring plan to avoid any delays.

Can you please let me know a couple dates/times next week that your schedule would permit a brief 15–20-minute call that I can share how we can help you with this?

Thank you,

Joe Smith
55-55-555
Business123

Now it's your turn. Put pen to paper and put this simple approach into action.

"Opportunity is missed by most people because it is dressed in overalls and looks like work." - Thomas Edison

We have been talking about e-mail for a while now, so let's bring it home.

Make sure you are using e-mail as one tool in your prospecting strategy. E-mail is not the only prospecting tool and relying on it as your only tool will only result in problems. Remember, just because you sent an e-mail doesn't actually mean you did anything. Do not be the person who sends an e-mail and then sits back and waits for a response that may never come.

Do not make your e-mail all about you and do not include a shopping list of everything you can do. I get it, you are awesome! The person you are reaching out to will get that eventually too. To start though focus each e-mail around one specific topic. Turning your e-mail into a shopping list is putting too much in front of the lead or prospect at once. Overwhelm them and they are not reading your e-mail, let alone responding.

When you create your e-mails keep in mind that it may (probably will) get read on someone's phone. As such, make sure it is readable on a phone. With that said, it does also need to be readable on a computer. You have to take both into account as you just don't know how your e-mail is going to be read.

Are you familiar with the mid-70's rock band KISS? They are kind of famous. They have nothing to do with e-mail, but KISS can also mean Keep It Stupid Simple (KISS). This applies to your e-mails. Keep them short and simple. They should be no more than 2 to 3 paragraphs as the person you are e-mail is much less likely to read long e-mails and even less likely to engage with you if the e-mail is long. Not everyone is like Beth, willing to wait at home until the boys find the sound. KISS!

Do not include any attachments or graphics in your initial outreach e-mails. Those can come later and can actually be a value add. Initially though, keep your e-mail clean to allow it to load quickly regardless of where it is being read and to prevent it from getting flagged as a risk in a spam filter. People are weary of attachments they aren't expecting. Get permission, then send your attachment.

Never ever, ever send the same e-mail twice to the same person. Repeat that with me – never ever, ever send the same e-mail twice to the same person. Just because you didn't receive a response does not mean the person didn't receive or read your e-mail. They probably did and they probably made a decision not to respond. You must always assume they read your e-mail. What do you think sending the same message twice says to the recipient? Is there any scenario that you come out in a positive light after sending the same e-mail to the same person multiple times? There is not. Do not do it. Do not be lazy. You are better than that!

"There are three kinds of men, ones that learn by reading, a few who learn by observation, and the rest of them have to pee on the electric fence and find out for themselves." - Will Rogers

Be sure to include a compelling subject line. People are looking for a reason to delete rather than read. Give them a reason to check out the content of your e-mail. Without a compelling subject line someone will find of interest you are inviting a high non-open rate. That does you no good.

After you catch their attention with your subject line and earn a small bit of the readers time, how do you ensure you don't lose them? Focus on the first 100 characters of your e-mail. These are extremely important. Think about it. Bad subject – your e-mail is not getting opened. Bad opening line – your e-mail is not getting read. It is like a stage gate process in which you need to continually earn the readers time and attention. It is up to you to ensure you don't lose them in any part of your e-mail. Make it compelling and be sure to add value.

I get it, you are really excited about helping the person you are trying to reach, but do not lose sight of the fact that they have a million and a half things on their plate. Even if you gave them a compelling reason to, and they want to get back to you, they may not be able to drop everything and do so. As such, never send more than four e-mails to the same contact over a six-week period without receiving a response. This minimizes the likelihood of your e-mail being tagged as spam by their e-mail filters. But more importantly, and again assuming they actually read your e-mail, the last thing you want to do is become a burden.

We will talk about prospecting plans and outreach cadence at some point, but considering a model in which you reach out once per week for four weeks straight (4x4). If after four weeks you still haven't received a response, reduce your cadence to every other week for the next four weeks (2x4). Then once in the next four-week period (1x4). This will ensure you are not pestering them. If you use this model, once you reduce your cadence to 2x4 find a new contact at the same company and start over with the 4x4 cadence.

Another one down. Now let's ensure what you read sticks. Let's take at least one (hopefully more) thing from this chapter and implement it to ensure the time you invested in reading this is beneficial. Here are some follow up activities to help do this.

– Infinite Positivity via E-mail Follow-Up Activities –

- Print the last 10 e-mails you have sent that didn't get a response and 10 e-mails that did. In each one, circle the elements of a strong e-mail; underline everything else. How do you stack up? Compare and see the differences of what worked and what did not.

- Write 10 sample subject lines designed to catch the prospects attention.

- Write 10 opening sentences to ensure the prospect will keep reading.

- Put this all together and write 10 sample e-mail scripts.

- Reread the summary at the end of this chapter and then compare your 10 sample scripts to the guidelines. How did they turn out? Are they better than the 10 you printed and circled/underlined?

"I am always doing that which I cannot do, in order that I may learn how to do it." - Pablo Picasso

Chapter Twelve

– A Day in the Life of Infinite Positivity –

Another reminder and example…

You have already seen a few of these, but here is a real-life example of Infinite Positivity in action to show how you can help your customers solve their challenges and transform your relationship from a transactional one, to a strategic partnership.

Here is another case study demonstrating what you should strive to achieve with your customers to help them solve a challenge. Once you do, who do you think they will call next time they find themself faced with a new challenge?

Case Study:

How we helped reallocate a customer's resources and refocused them on achieving their mission

Background:

The customer, a contract development and manufacturing organization (CDMO) and cancer research center working in the ever and rapidly evolving cell and gene therapy industry was using Glycerin as part of their upstream cell culture process.

Challenge:

The Glycerin the customer was purchasing was from a well-known life science catalog company and it was a bulk off-the-shelf product for them. As per the customer's upstream cell culture processing, they needed to dilute the Glycerin and once diluted, to avoid impacting their cells, they needed it to be sterilized. The customer had established a process to process the bulk Glycerin into their cleanroom, to perform the dilution, to fill it into the 10L units their process required, and to complete a post-manufacturing sterilization step. This process was not aligned with their core capabilities, nor did it support their mission to eliminate cancer and related diseases as causes of human suffering and death. Rather it was creating excess work and taking them away from more important activities.

Solution:

We partnered with the customer to understand their process and their needs. After obtaining a thorough understanding, we transferred their entire process to our company whose expertise was in sterile, reagent manufacturing. We sourced the bulk Glycerin, the packaging, and everything else needed to support the process. We performed the dilution and filling into the 10L configuration. We performed the post-manufacturing sterilization. All of this allowed us to deliver a ready-to-use solution aligned precisely to their needs, utilizing the process they established. In doing so, we eliminated multiple steps from their existing process, saving numerous employee hours for them; hours they could reallocate to more important activities that truly helped them support their very meaningful and impactful mission or eliminating cancer.

I support that. Who would not want a company like this focusing more on eliminating cancer? Based on this case study, we were able to help them accomplish this. Not just a win for Infinite Positivity, but a win for humanity!

Let's keep going!

"The only difference between successful people and non-successful people is this: everybody thinks about what they want, but successful people think about what they want, and HOW to get it." - Brian Tracy

Chapter Thirteen

– Infinite Positivity via Social Media –

Let's get social.

Social media sites, and for that matter, the entire Internet, provides the ability to create a digital trail that anyone can access 24/7. As such, it is of vital importance to realize your profile and your activity on social media sites is picked up by search engines, and for most people these sites will pop up the highest in a quick Google search of your name. Your profile and your activity say something about it; it is your personal brand.

A positive personal brand is the easiest way to earn more confidence with your customers and prospects, and even generate leads, when done right. Remember - the more confidence the customer has in us, the greater probability we have of earning their business. For this reason, it is critical to cultivate a positive personal brand. As you live the Infinite Positivity model, this should not be an issue for you.

I am not going to cover how to do this, but I would recommend reading Up your Game by David Bradford and/or The Zen of Social Media Marketing by Shama Hyder for help accomplishing this. Both are great reads with lots of information and tips on how to cultivate your positive brand. Check them out!

Now back to getting social - consider social media the same as live networking events. Why you ask. Many times, the audience is the same from event to event. This repetition is certainly a good thing, as it is a key element to a prospecting programs success. The challenge comes from the impact we can have using social media as it can take a significant amount of time to build a large enough presence on social media sites to make a difference. Combine this with how long it can take prospects to see your value, which I will explain in a moment, too much investment in social media can be a misuse of your time.

There may be people who disagree with me on this, but the big concern is time. As we have talked about, the only asset that is limited in business is time, specifically your time. Spending hours a day on social media sites might give you a rush when seeing the number of likes, followers, and connections, but these have little value unless you convert them into customers. One of the worst things we can believe is that all of our social media connections are leads just waiting to become customers. They are not. You need to understand and accept the reality that a lot of our connections have no potential to ever become prospects.

As such, the time you spend on social media must be time you would not spend on more productive prospecting activities! Social media sites are full of distractions that will pull you away from more productive work. Scrolling through your feed is probably not going to result in you adding new customers. Also, most social media activities do not occur in real time. You do not post something and then instantly get to have a conversation with someone. Sure, there are exceptions, but most people do not live on social media sites waiting for you to connect with them.

"The biggest communication problem is we do not listen to understand. We listen to reply." - Stephen R. Covey

When using social media, you need to keep in mind that people will probably not respond in a timely manner. It's easy for us in sales to think that because we are on social media sites such as LinkedIn, everyone is. The majority of people who are active on LinkedIn fall in one of three broad categories: salespeople, HR, or people in employment transitions.

Mid-level managers and others you are targeting may only check social media sites once a week or once a month. If your target is the C-suite, you may not find them active on social media at all. Of course there are always exceptions to the rule. By no means does this mean social media sites can't get you to your targets; it just means you may need to reach them by going through someone else that knows them that you are connected to.

Facebook, X, Instagram, Pinterest, and other social media sites all have different target audiences as well. How you feel about these sites is not what matters. What matters is what the person you are trying to connect with thinks of them. Remember - this is not about you.

So how and why do we use social media to prospect then?

It allows you to communicate directly with your prospects. This is by far the most effective way to prospect, as you are reaching out to build communication with the person you have identified as a potential prospect.

It allows you to connect with people who can connect you with other people you are trying to reach. For many salespeople, this can be the only way to connect with your target if they are not on social media. With this approach, you are reaching out and communicating with people who can connect you with your target.

It allows you to see who is looking at your profile so you can respond to the people inquiring about you. This is where a bigger social footprint comes in and offers the potential to generate more opportunities. Big opportunities can come from people sending you messages via LinkedIn and X or people viewing your profile. They are doing so for a reason. It is your job to find out what that reason is.

"If you want to win in the 21st century, you have to empower others, making sure other people are better than you. Then you will be successful." - Jack Ma

Finding potential leads begins with monitoring who views your profile. Pay attention to who is viewing your profile, and if you see any potential leads, reach out to them immediately. Some might say this is aggressive, but if you believe what you do can help others, then you owe it to them to connect. And again, they are looking at your profile for a reason. They saw something of interest. Find out what that was.

How you reach out to them will vary based on what the social media site allows you to do. The preferred way is to ask for a connection and message them within the site structure to engage them in a conversation.

When you connect with someone you must keep in mind the "social" aspect of social media. Many people on social media are on there to build their network and to be social. I doubt anyone is on social media to be sold to. As such you must keep in mind a crucial rule.

Never ever try to sell until a relationship is established. Just because someone accepts your invitation to connect does not mean you turn around and ask them to buy from you. You must provide value, you must establish a relationship, you must earn the opportunity to sell to them. This may sound like common sense, but I cannot tell you how often this happens. You would never do this in real life, so you should never do it over social media. Do not be that person.

"Always start a relationship by asking: Do I have ulterior motives for wanting to relate to this person? Is my caring conditional? Am I trying to escape something? Am I planning to change the person? Do I need this person to help me make up for a deficiency in myself? If your answer to any of these questions is 'yes,' leave the person alone. He or she is better off without you." - Leo Buscaglia

What should the process of social selling look like?

It is best to keep your communication via social media "social" in nature at first. As per the critical rule, never send an initial message to someone with a direct request to uncover in immediate business need. Instead, consider an initial message in which you ask them a question or make a comment about something the two of you have in common. Then it is up to them to make the next move, and with social media we have to be patient as that next move may not occur for a while.

Depending on how the person responds determines your next step. At this point, be sure to keep your response focused on what they sent you in their response. After a second response you can start to move forward and begin to shift the discussion to a topic that allows you to uncover a need you can help them with.

Once the conversation moves in this direction, you should also try to move it "offline" from the social media site. This is also an easy way to begin qualifying the contact and seeing if they could be a prospect, or if they are just someone looking to be social. Someone who is willing to move the discussion to e-mail or phone certainly expresses some interest. Someone who does not want to move away from the social media site may still be a viable lead, but it may take more time to be certain.

As with the phone calls, the voicemails, and the e-mails we have already talked about, you need to be sure to record your social media activities in your CRM system. You don't want to lose credibility by not remembering what you did or said weeks or months earlier when you finally do communicate with your target.

This simple approach will allow you to provide value, to establish a relationship, and to earn the opportunity to sell to them. That is Infinite Positivity!

"One of the best ways to persuade others is with your ears – by listening to them." - Dean Rusk

Search, seek, and connect.

Groups and group postings are another way to uncover potential leads, especially if you are a member of a technical or support group. Other members post challenges and questions they are faced with looking for help. That sounds like a perfect segway for you to connect with them – to help them.

If you are creating posts for the group, unlike when you are targeting specific people, you want to keep the post more general to fit a broader profile of prospects. Contacting group members and responding to group posts is an activity that should be relegated to weekends or in the evening when your time cannot be spent on more productive sales activities.

Uncovering prospects via social media groups can be time-consuming, and salespeople can only do it if they can control themselves from spending too much time on social media sites. Don't get stuck scrolling your time away.

As we talked about previously, if someone who receives the group message responds to you, use the same approach you would with direct prospects - reply back with another comment or question that builds on the first. The second response you received from them can then be your guide to know if they're worth pursuing.

Another benefit that can be found in LinkedIn groups is that if you are unable to send a message to a prospect since you are not connected with them; if you are a member of one of the same groups as them, you can message them directly as a result of sharing that link.

Another high return activity when identifying potential leads is doing keyword searches of job titles or company names. LinkedIn search for people should be your best friend. Master it as it can play a huge and valuable role in your prospecting efforts.

Never underestimate the search engine capabilities of a social media site to help uncover new opportunities. Your ability to connect with any leads you identify will be driven by the parameters set by the social media site, but typically there is some method you can use to contact them.

As with the other social media strategies, the approach is to make the initial message a question or a comment about something they find a value.

Because we are talking about social media, a response could come in five minutes or five weeks. Do not take the speed of the response as an indication of interest. Response time is more often driven by how often the person you are trying to contact looks at the social media site and/or the settings they have created to receive messages (which e-mail address their notifications go to).

"The way we spend our time defines who we are." - Jonathan Estrin

This one is a shorter chapter than the others. Not because social media is not a tool you should use in your prospecting (you should use it), but because of the pitfalls and time suck it can have on you. Start slow and then scale your time on social media based on positive outcomes. Additional time should be earned based on results.

Consider starting with one hour per week. You can break this hour into three 20 minutes segments each week: two on weeknights and the third sometimes during the weekend. Breaking up your one hour over three separate occasions will give you more than enough time to post, comment, share, and connect. What it won't do is give you enough time to wander around watching stupid cat videos! Sorry to be the bearer of bad news but watching cat videos is not going to find you business.

Let's bring it home on social media. You should be used to this by now, but let's ensure what you read sticks. Let's take at least one (hopefully more) thing from this chapter and implement it to ensure the time you invested in reading this is beneficial. Here are some follow up activities to help do this.

— Infinite Positivity via Social Media Follow-Up Activities —

- Update your social media profile(s) to ensure they Stand Up and speak of integrity.

- Start Up and for the next 48 hours talk to people everywhere you go. Learn what each person's story is that you talk with. Then Follow Up with them all within 24 hours in some form or another.

- Contact 10 people in your network you haven't connected with in the last 6 months. Then contact 20 more people in your network you haven't connected with in the last year. Show genuine interest and be sure to add value to Show Up.

- Reach out to 5 people you haven't met over social media to Link Up. Be sure to include a personal note to each person about why you choose them and not a generic invite.

- Remember networking is like preparing for any athletic contest; it requires consistent and daily work on the effort to Scale Up. Schedule 10-15 minutes a day to work on your network until it becomes a habit.

"The capacity to care is what gives life its most deepest significance." - Pablo Casals

Chapter Fourteen

– Focus on the Big 3 –

Rather than sharing a case study between chapters as we have been doing, I want to change it up a bit and introduce you to the Big 3.

Remember this is Infinite Positivity which is all about helping those you are selling to, leaving them and their situation better as a result of your involvement as when you accomplish what is most important to them, you earn trust and credibility, establishing the foundation for a long-term partnership of success.

The Big 3 is a means to accomplish this. The first time I heard of the Big 3 was a few years back working with a gentleman named Aaron Benz. Mr. Benz, as I came to call my friend and colleague, shared this simple model with me and I have benefited from it ever since. Now I am going to share it with you.

This chapter focuses on the Big 3.

By the end it, you will understand what the Big 3 are, why they matter, and you will also understand how to address them through the information shared in the case studies included (I know we said we weren't doing case studies – you get a bonus).

This chapter will conclude with how you can use outsourcing as a means to achieve them, not to mention simplifying the customers process and supply chain, to make their life easier and to allow them to focus on what they do best. In other words, adding significant value to the customer by helping them to improve their situation while accomplishing what is most important to them.

"Stop being patient and start asking yourself, how do I accomplish my 10-year plan in 6 months? You'll probably fail, but you'll be a lot further along than the person who simply accepts it was going to take 10 years." - Elon Musk

So, what are the Big 3? For as long as I can recall in most businesses and industries, almost every corporate activity deployed ties back to achieving goals within the Big 3. They are high level strategic goals every company is measuring in some way, shape, or form.

These goals are…

- Increasing revenue generation

- Reducing cost

- Mitigating risk

Your next question should be, how can Infinite Positivity help achieve goals in each of these areas. Good question! I am glad you asked.

Every company wants to grow, increase revenue generation, and gain market share. One of the primary challenges today is the speed in which new technologies or products are developed and commercialized. This in turn drastically shortens the lifecycle of a technology or product. Therefore, speed to market is crucial to revenue generation and market share gains.

Many companies have embraced the idea of outsourcing the scale-up and commercialization of new and existing products as choosing this strategy allows them to reallocate internal resources to developing the next great technology. This strategy has proven to be successful for increasing revenue generation and aggressively attacking market share within the same market segment and developing products for adjacent or new market segments.

Increasing revenue generation is meaningless if a company loses gross margin dollars; this is where reducing cost comes into play.

Cost reduction is another challenge companies are forced to address. Labor, overhead, raw materials, process improvement, and packaging are just a few of the areas companies have seen significant cost increases. A good partner can directly reduce these costs and help a company yield higher gross margin dollars. Leveraging scales of economy for raw materials, packaging, increased manufacturing lot sizes, and application of automation to dilute the cost per unit to manufacture a product can yield lower labor costs, overhead, and warehousing depending on the geographic location of the partner.

All of these categories are opportunities for cost reduction ultimately resulting in significantly higher gross margin dollars.

Corporate risk is lurking everywhere - employee liability, facility contingency planning, product consistency, and product quality.

A good partner offers an opportunity to mitigate risk across a broad spectrum of business challenges, especially if that partner can provide manufacturing redundancy by manufacturing a portion of the volume of a product to ensure the customer can still operate in the event of a catastrophic event. Doing so can also offer significant increases to product consistency through manufacturing automation, as well as by eliminating the human error factor from a process to provide a more consistent quality product because every action is performed identically.

These examples mitigate the risk of both potential lost revenue and the cost of potential product failure.

Embracing the philosophy of outsourcing in the constantly changing world has become the method of choice to accelerate revenue growth and market share gains, successfully reduce costs to increase gross margin dollars, and to mitigate corporate risk that continues to grow.

How do you do this? What does this look like?

"Let us make our future now and let us make our dreams tomorrow's reality." - Malala Yousafzai

What follows are a few examples of what this can entail.

First, there are three real life case studies that demonstrate this process. These are case studies based on actual life science and biotech companies. For obvious reasons, their names have been omitted from what follows; however, the challenges, the needs, the solutions all occurred.

Once the case studies are completed, I will then walk through how and what to look for as your customers develop products and as they move them through their product lifecycle to further demonstrate this process.

All of this should provide you with some tips and tricks regarding what to look for so you can help your customers achieve the Big 3.

Case Study # 1 –

- Customer A.

- Proprietary liquid buffer they formulate internally.

- Source the raw materials to formulate.

- Industry standard packaging for these raw materials is paper bags.

- Formulation occurs in a cleanroom.

- Industry standard pack sizes do not align with their formulation.

- Devote time and resources to issuance (weighing) and re-packaging the raw materials to process them into their cleanroom.

- Need help.

What can you do to help?

While this information is limited, think about it. How would you approach helping this customer? Please take a moment and put pen to paper. Write out what you think you could do to achieve the Big 3.

"Be the change that you wish to see in the world." - Mahatma Gandhi

What to know what actually happened? Let me fill in the gaps and walk you through the outcome.

Customer A formulates a buffer they use as part of their manufacturing process internally. It is a proprietary formulation, and they are not comfortable disclosing it, so they are left with having to formulate it themselves. They source the necessary powdered raw materials used in that formulation from their current vendor and the materials are received in paper bags. They manufacture in a cleanroom and are unable to process paper bags into their cleanrooms as a result of potential microbial contamination. Because of this, they have to repack the powdered materials into different packaging in order to process them into their cleanrooms. Once inside they also spend a good deal of time on issuance of the powdered materials as the pack sizes of the powdered materials do not align with their formulation and the scale they are manufacturing. As a result, they are forced to combine multiple units of each material as per the pack sizes available from the supplier.

There has to be a better way, right?

In this scenario, we were able to work with Customer A to determine pack sizes based on their actual utilization of the raw materials and we were able to right size the pack sizes to align with that. Meaning we did away with the industry standard pack sizes and filled exactly to what their process needed. We also added weights to the labels of each unit of raw material we provided that were reported out to the third decimal point thus eliminating the need for them devoting their time and resources to issuance. We also were able to pack each raw material double bagged in lined plastic drums which meant they no longer had to re-package the material just to process it into their cleanrooms. In making these minor modifications in their supply chain, we were able to make their manufacturing process quicker and more efficient by providing them with a ready-to-use option, thus achieving two of the big three – improvement in gross margins and risk mitigation.

How does that align with what you put on paper?

"If you're not making mistakes, then you're not doing anything. I'm positive that a doer makes mistakes." - John Wooden

Let's do another.

Case Study # 2 –

- Customer B.

- Diagnostic manufacturer.

- Launched a NEW product.

- Based in California.

- Limited resources – both staff and financial.

- Scaling to commercialization.

- Need help.

How can you help them?

Same as the last one. While this information is limited, think about it and put pen to paper. Write out what you think you could do to help Customer B and to address the big 3.

Want to know what actually happened?

Customer B manufactures a diagnostic and just received FDA approval for a new product, a diagnostic kit. Their technology is the actual diagnostic portion of the product, and they outsource the manufacturing of the packaging and reagents that accompany their technology in the kit. To obtain market approval, all of the kits they made were assembled by their entire team. Once a week they would call everyone together (their senior management, their PhD scientists, everyone) and they would create an assembly line of sorts in one of their conference rooms to assemble the kits. They are based in California and do not have the infrastructure, financial resources, staff, or space in their facility to scale up both the manufacturing of their technology and the kitting to support the commercialization of their new product.

If only there were a solution. As a result of their situation, we were able to help them decide to look for a partner to help them with the kitting portion as that is the most manual intensive portion of the process and easiest to outsource. We were able to help them determine that in order to make the process work they need to reallocate their teams time and energy away from the sourcing of the reagents going into the kits, as well as the assembly of those kits, back to the actual manufacturing of their technology. We were able to transfer their entire kitting process from California to a state with a much lower cost of living, which reduced the cost. This included sourcing and replicating their printed boxes, the instructions for use, the package inserts, as well as all the reagents and consumables that go in the kit. We established a mutually agreed upon protocol/procedure for assembling the kits, complete with their required QC inspection process, to manufacture and store their kits at our facility, and drop ship the assembled and ready to use kits anywhere in the world they needed them to be sent.

All of this allowed them to focus on what they do best, which was manufacture their technology. It also allowed them to simplify their supply chain as they were able to go from managing multiple suppliers for their packaging, reagents, and everything else to a single supplier that managed that entire process for them. In addition, they were also able to save space in their facility by not having to hold inventory of the kitting materials and final product ready for distribution. Their cost savings from moving all of these activities out of their facility in California to ours were also significant, thus improving gross margins.

How did you do? Is that what you came up with as a solution to their challenge too?

"You're going to go through tough times – that's life. But I say, 'nothing happens to you, it happens for you.' See the positive in negative events." - Joel Osteen

Last one. Again, put pen to paper and see if you can solve the challenge.

Case Study # 3 –

- Customer C.

- Biologic manufacturer.

- Aseptic manufacturing process entailing a series of washes, rinses, and soaks in various liquid chemicals.

- Industry standard fill volumes, concentrations, and fill volumes for liquid chemicals.

- Supply of liquid chemicals is critical.

- Disruption in their ability to process is incredibly costly for them.

- Limited storage space at facility for liquid chemicals.

- Need help.

What do you do to help? What do you think?

Customer C is one of 48 manufactures in the US that utilizes a very similar aseptic manufacturing process for a biologic that entails a series of washes, rinses, and soaks in various reagents. While the process between these 48 manufacturers is similar each manufacturer utilizes slightly different concentrations, soak times, and volumes. However, as a result of the standardization between these 48 manufactures the current reagent suppliers for this industry have standardized their offering based on the most common fill volumes and concentrations used.

It is also important to note that because Customer C is manufacturing a biologic, if they do not have the necessary reagents for their manufacturing process they cannot proceed and will be forced to discard the biological material, which is not only wasteful, but extremely costly for them.

They spend a lot of their time managing this and their supply chain and have to balance this with limited warehousing capacity. Hopefully you can start to see where we are going with this.

The first thing we were able to do was similar to what we shared in the first case study in that we were able to right size their volumes with their actual process to eliminate waste or utilizing multiple units of the reagents by providing them with a single unit filled to align with their specific process. We were also able to work with them to provide the concentrations and specifications of these reagents that their process required. In addition, we were able to understand their usage of these reagents to manufacture a six-month stock for them as a single lot. We set up a shipping schedule in which twice a month like clockwork, we would send Customer C a predetermined and mutually agreed upon quantity of each reagent that was based on their actual processing. This shipping schedule allowed them to maintain a month's stock of these critical reagents at their facility and it allowed us to maintain at least three months stock at our facility that was allocated for only them. We established par levels that we would replenish those reagents once we dipped below the three-month stock level at our facility as well.

In doing all of this, it allowed us to provide them with a guaranteed stock of the reagents they needed to avoid any potential disruptions. It provided them a safety net. It also allowed them to receive and use these reagents just how they needed to in order to optimize their process, thus achieving cost savings, improving gross margins, and mitigating risk. This also allowed us to reduce their warehousing space, which in turn they were able to reallocate to expanding their finished goods inventory which is a revenue generating activity.

Is that what you wrote down? That is why they say, "great minds think alike."

Hopefully those case studies help illustrate what achieving the Big 3 could entail.

"Thinking is hard work; that's why so few do it." - John C. Maxwell

Let's look at it from a different angle now.

You just developed a new product. Congratulations! It is an exciting time. But what do you do now? According to Harvard Business School professor Clayton Christensen, each year more than 30,000 new consumer products are launched. That is consumer products and not the products that originate in academia, research and development labs, or the product development labs that ultimately feed into the life science and biotech industries we are talking about. This is where I have spent my career, so that is where most of my examples come from. This number of new products launched is interesting and tells us that there are new ideas flowing into the market every day. What is more interesting about this number is that 95% of them fail. A lot of time and effort goes into developing a new product. The last thing you want is for yours to be added to the majority and for it not to get out of the gate. You want yours to be part of the 5% that go on to the market and become successful.

In order to set your product up for success and to be part of that 5%, the first step is to scale up your process. Rarely is it easy to scale from the small-scale development work you did on a benchtop in a laboratory, to a large-scale manufacturing process in an FDA regulated, quality driven, manufacturing facility. These two environments are nowhere close to the same.

Most of the time you will have to take a hard look at and, in some cases, make changes to your process, as what you do in a lab is simply different than what is done in production for a variety of reasons. What do you need to consider?

Your equipment, as the equipment used at each phase in the process is different based on the desired outcome.

Your materials, as purchasing in milligrams or milliliters to support the development at a small scale may work perfect, but what happens when you need to scale to hundreds of kilograms or liters? Are you going to allocate your resources to opening thousands of milligram or milliliter units? Are you even able to get the same material with the same specifications from the same manufacturer at production quantities, or will you have to requalify and revalidate?

Your people, as you may be the only one to have successfully manufactured this product to date. Do you have a robust enough process and/or procedure to transfer it so someone else can replicate what you did?

Your facility, as you may not have the equipment, capacity, space, or QA/RA certifications/approvals to manufacture a medical device, a diagnostic, a biologic, or a drug in your current facility and correcting this could result in a lengthy process and substantial investment in infrastructure.

Your formulations, as what you did on the benchtop may not scale the way you intend it to. This could take on a variety of different forms from pH adjustments, to chemicals not blending the same, to unanticipated alterations to specifications, as simply multiplying what you did on the benchtop by 100X doesn't always produce the same outcome.

Hopefully you get the gist of it at this point that scaling up a process isn't easy.

"It is not enough to do your best; you must know what to do, and THEN do your best." - W. Edwards Deming

What about transferring your process then?

Technology (tech) transfer is the process of disseminating skills, knowledge, technologies, manufacturing methods, samples, and facilities among the participants. These transfers may occur between universities, businesses, (of any size, ranging from small, medium, to large), departments (R&D or development to operations), both formally and informally.

This is done to ensure that scientific and technological developments are accessible to a wider range of users who can then further develop and exploit the technology into new products, processes, applications, materials, or services, as well as to allow the technology to reach a larger customer base.

Some companies have entire departments focused on this process. Others have a proceduralized way to do this. Regardless of what is in place, it is a much-needed part of the process that needs to occur and a problem that must be solved.

As such, if you take a strategic approach to the process considering what you found when you took a hard look at your process and considered some of the scale up matters we just covered, you can eliminate some potential hurdles and challenges in this process to make your customers life and this process easier.

While I wish I could tell you there is a secret sauce, or a one-size-fits-all solution, a mythical silver bullet, that will quickly and easily make all of this just go away, unfortunately, there isn't one.

Your customer will need to address some of the matters we covered, and it will take hard work to do so as ultimately, they have responsibility for their product and ultimately, they are accountable for it from a quality and regulatory liability standpoint. But, with that said, they don't have to do everything on their own. They don't have to recreate the wheel. You can help them!

"There are no secrets to success. It is the result of preparation, hard work, and learning from failure." - Colin Powell

By achieving the Big 3 you can help them to realize their market aspirations.

You can help them take their product from small scale to benchtop to production scale.

You can provide them guidance on quality, regulatory, and facility requirements.

You can scale with them regarding their raw materials to eliminate the need for having to revalidate different raw materials.

You can help them right size how they receive their raw materials based on their specific application to gain efficiencies in their process.

You can help them establish redundancy with both their manufacturing and their supply chain.

You can help them focus their resources where they belong and on what they do best. You can help them get to market faster.

You can help them to reduce their cost per unit through larger scales of economies.

You can help them lower their labor costs, their overhead, and warehousing costs through outsourcing their manufacturing, warehousing, and shipping.

You can help prevent and eliminate unnecessary infrastructure investments. You can help them increase product consistency by adding manufacturing and fill/finish automation.

I am sure you get the point, but this list goes on and on. You can simply help them. That is what Infinite Positivity is all about.

"Success is no accident. It is hard work, perseverance, learning, studying, sacrifice and most of all, love of what you are doing or learning to do." - Pele

What we are talking about doesn't only apply to new products. It also applies to existing and mature products. Think about your customers and what they are doing, their processes. Consider asking...

Do they manufacture their own reagents to use in that process? If so, who does that? Is it a scientist or a supervisor that they would benefit from reallocating their time to something else?

Do they spend time on issuance weighing out materials before they are able to proceed with the manufacturing process? Would it make them more efficient to have pre-weighed and labeled weights on each of their raw materials reported out three decimal places?

Do they have to open multiple raw material units in order to get to the quantity they need? For example, does their process require them to use 10Kgs, but they buy it in 1Kgs containers as that is what is commonly available on the market, and they then open all ten units to combine them into one to support their manufacturing. Would it not be easier to have a ready to use 10Kgs pack size for that material?

Is their facility set up to manufacture their technology, which is one component of a kit, and they have to source all of the other components and then as time permits assemble the kits? Would they not be more efficient if they focused their attention on their technology, what they do best, and found a partner to manage the rest of that process for them as part of their custom kitting capabilities?

In that same scenario, if they do not have a work cell established for this process but rather pull in various members of their team including scientists, supervisors, management etc., would they not be able to benefit from some cost savings by having someone that has established work centers staffed with experienced hourly workers.

Taking this thought one step further, consider if they do this in Irvine, San Francisco, or Boston where the cost of living and the associated salaries of those involved are high. What if they were to move that labor to another state with a lower cost of living and therefore lower salary rate. Again, wouldn't they benefit from some cost savings.

What would they then be able to do with the space that process was taking up as they reallocate it to other activities possibly including the development of their next product or the gen 2 version of their current product. At this point they would have lowered their overhead to manufacture their product as well based on real estate costs in California or Massachusetts versus other states. More cost savings.

These are all just some of the ways they can gain efficiency in their current processes by simply asking questions.

Did you notice not once in any of this did I mention a product? That is because with Infinite Positivity you are not selling a product; you are helping them find a better, more efficient way.

"If you do not know how to ask the right question, you discover nothing." - William Edwards Demming

This chapter on the Big 3 has covered a lot of material, so let's bring it all together.

As we discussed, almost every corporate activity deployed ties back to achieving goals within the Big 3, which are high level strategic goals that every company is measuring in some way, shape, or form. These goals are increasing revenue generation, reducing cost, and mitigating risk.

We broke down each of these goals and identified a common solution pertaining to outsourcing, as in the constantly changing world of business it has becoming the method of choice to accelerate revenue growth and market share gains, successfully reduce costs to increase gross margin dollars, and to mitigate corporate risk that continues to grow.

We took this one step further and walked through some real-life examples of what doing so could look like and after that we put product development and scaling up to commercialization under that same lens and walked through some examples of what those entail. We did the same for established manufacturing processes as a means to drive continuous improvements and to achieve the Big 3.

Most of this entailed understanding your customers' products, where they are in their lifecycle, and their processes and asking questions about how they could do things better, more efficiently, easier. Then taking what those questions unearthed and finding creative solutions to help them address them, so they too can accomplish their goals and achieve the Big 3.

Now that you understand the Big 3, it is up to you to convince your customers to let you help them achieve them. You've got this!

"The life that is not examined is not worth living." - Plato

Before concluding this chapter, a few years ago I convinced Mr. Benz to pen an article on the Big 3. What follows is his original article in its entirety. I appreciate you sharing the Big 3 with me, my friend. Now I feel fortunate to pass it along so others can benefit as I have.

"In recent years in the life science and biotech chemical manufacturing industries, almost every corporate activity deployed ties back to achieving goals within the Big 3. So, what is the Big 3? They are high level strategic goals that every company is measuring in some way, shape, or form. These goals are increasing revenue generation, reducing cost, and mitigating risk. Your next question should be, how can outsourcing help achieve goals in each of these areas.

Every company wants to grow, increase revenue generation, and gain market share. One of the primary challenges in today's life science and biotech industries is the speed in which new technologies or products are developed and commercialized. This in turn drastically shortens the lifecycle of a technology or product. Therefore, speed to market is crucial to revenue generation and market share gains. Many companies have embraced the idea of outsourcing the scale-up and commercialization of new products as choosing this strategy allows companies to re-allocate internal resources to developing the next great technology while leveraging a good contract development and manufacturing organization (CDMO) to do the heavy lifting of the actual manufacturing. This strategy has proved to be successful for increasing revenue generation and aggressively attacking market share.

Increasing revenue generation is meaningless if a company loses gross margin dollars; this is where reducing cost comes into play. Cost reduction is another challenge companies are forced to address. Labor, overhead, raw materials and packaging are just a few of the areas that companies have seen significant cost increases. A good CDMO partner can directly reduce these costs and help a company yield higher gross margin dollars. CDMO's can leverage scales of economy for raw materials, packaging, increased manufacturing lot sizes, and application of automation to dilute the cost per unit to manufacture a product. Leveraging a CDMO partner can yield lower labor costs, overhead, and warehousing depending on the geographic location of the partner. All of these categories are opportunities for cost reduction ultimately resulting in significantly higher gross margin dollars.

Corporate risk is lurking everywhere - employee liability, facility contingency planning, product consistency, and product quality. CDMO's offer their clientele an opportunity to mitigate risk across a broad spectrum of business challenges. CDMO partners can provide a customer manufacturing redundancy by manufacturing a portion of the volume of a product to ensure the customer can still operate in the event of a catastrophic event. A CDMO can also offer significant increases to product consistency through manufacturing and fill/finish automation. Eliminating the human error factor from a process has been demonstrated to provide a more consistent quality product because every action is performed identically. These examples mitigate the risk of both potential lost revenue and the cost of potential product failure.

Embracing the philosophy of outsourcing in the constantly changing life science and biotech industries is quickly becoming the method of choice to accelerate revenue growth and market share gains, successfully reduce costs to increase gross margin dollars, and to mitigate corporate risk that continues to grow."

"Count today a privilege to be able to learn from those you meet and share with those you care about." - Mark Hunter

Chapter Fifteen

– Your Infinite Positivity Plan –

We are nearly there! It is time to bring all of the prospecting stuff we have been talking about together.

Before you compile your prospecting plan, there are a few more things to cover and a few more tips to share.

At the end of this chapter, you will have everything you need to compile and execute a successful prospecting plan.

What is the one thing all companies have in common?

Global giants and the smallest of companies are all comprised of people. The only difference is the number of zeros in their yearly results and the set of rules by which they play.

Everything you have read so far focuses on helping people, so what we have covered will work with even the largest of companies. But you need to approach them a little differently. When prospecting big companies, it is all about earned time.

What do I mean by earned time? Your goal is to find out as quickly as possible the answers to these questions:

- What are the goals/objectives they need to accomplish?

- What barriers are they facing?

- What is the timeline they operate under?

- Where is the power within the company?

- What is the company's tolerance for risk?

That is it. There is no need to overcomplicate things.

The challenge for you will be finding the right people who can and will help you uncover the answers to these questions, because only when you have answers will you know how to assist them.

Another of your goals is to avoid being routed to Purchasing. Nothing against people in the fine profession of Purchasing, but just like you are trained to sell, they are trained to buy – what they want, when they want. As such, if all you are looking for is a quote request then go ahead and go directly to Purchasing but know you will most likely be selling on price at that point which will make it difficult to earn the business.

Your best chance is to find people in an organization who will answer your questions and fill one of the critical roles in the customer buying process.

"Give yourself permission to live a big life. Step into who you are meant to be. Stop playing small. You're meant for greater things." - Carlii Lyon

Each person you connect with in search of the answers to the aforementioned questions will most likely fill one of seven standard roles in the buying process. It is important to understand these roles as each of them want and need something different. Sounds like a great opportunity to help multiple people if you ask me! So, what are these roles:

-Users: The person who actually uses what you sell. What a fantastic source of information!

- Owner: The person who owns the budget that will provide the funds to purchase. Usually the Users supervisor. While they may not have the day to day experience the user does, they are still familiar enough to provide valuable information.

- Decision Maker: The person who owns the decision-making process. This could be the Owner, or it could be someone further up the food chain. You may also find there is not a sole Decision Maker, but a buying committee full of Decision Makers. This or these are critical people to know otherwise you may not be able to influence the decision in the end.

- Champion: The person who works on your behalf to advance the process. This is usually someone who is completely bought in to the solution you are selling; whether it will have a significant positive effect on them personally, or they have benefitted from using your solution elsewhere, they are as good as on your team. This is someone willing to speak out and put their neck on the line to vouch for you. These people are as good as gold.

- Influencer: The person who wants to be involved in the decision-making process. Ever heard of a circle of trust or an inner circle? There are people who will impact the final decision even if the outcome has nothing to do with them. These people are simply trusted resources to the other roles. What if you were to influence the Influencer?

- Optimizer: The person who is proactive in finding ways to create better outcomes. Usually an eternal optimist who always believes there is a better way to do something, Optimizers want continuous improvement. They live for it and will sometimes do anything to achieve it, maybe even by becoming a Champion.

-Road Blocker: The person who, usually for their own gain, will attempt to sabotage or block a decision. This could be the person responsible for putting what your solution will replace in place. They could be someone adverse to risk. They could be someone about to retire or leave the company that doesn't want to put in the extra work that comes with a change. They could just be someone in a bad mood. Whatever their motivation the sooner you can identify these people the better you can determine how to avoid them.

These types of people will not exist in every situation; however, the larger the company or the larger the project, the greater the number of people who will be looking to play a role in the decision.

Your goal is to understand what position your contact is in and, as opportunities arise, identify and engage others in the company to fill the other roles.

"Some people look for a beautiful place. Others make a place beautiful." - Hazrat Inayat Khan

A few more thoughts on selling to large companies.

Always ask at the end of any conversation if there is someone else in the company who also can give you input. Try using phrases like, I was curious about, or I am confused by, and then ask who can help you better understand. This is a means to expand your reach, contacts, and understanding in the company.

How they have made similar buying decisions in the past, including budgeting issues, timelines, contract requirements, vendor approvals, and bidding processes? Unless you have worked with them in the past and have firsthand experience with this, ask them. That is the only way you will find out. Otherwise you will be guessing throughout the entire process. You do not want that, so ask. The earlier you know this information, the better you will understand timelines, processes, and how to move things forward.

With each new contact you get, regardless of the number of contacts you have within a company, keep them engaged via e-mail. Send them e-mails containing key information about the industry, a competitor, or other relevant insights you have learned about them. If you can become a trusted source of value, even when they do not have an immediate need, who do you think they will come to when they do have a need? Do not send them a single e-mail when you meet them and think you are good. Engage them enough so they see you as a valued resource with great information.

What do you do when you receive an Out of Office (OOO) e-mail? Do you delete it? What about when you see a new contact copied (cc'd) on an e-mail? Ignore them, respond, and file the e-mail? If so, you are missing out. OOO responses usually contain contact information for someone you can contact for immediate assistance. Sometimes they contain lists of contacts and outline the responsibilities of each contact. Congratulations! You just earned a free introduction to a new contact. Take it. Contact them. Same with each person cc'd on an e-mail. They are on there for a reason. You need to figure out why, so you can help them. E-mail them and introduce yourself. You literally have nothing to lose as they are already familiar with you and what you are working on. They could be a new source of information, or they could fill one of the roles we talked about. You never know until you try.

"Stay positive and happy. Work hard and don't give up hope. Be open to criticism and keep learning. Surround yourself with happy, warm and genuine people." - Tena Desae

If you start talking with someone at your target company in a different department and they attempt to push you to Purchasing tell them, "We will absolutely want to involve your Purchasing team, but before we do so there are still a few more things for us to clarify in order to make those conversation productive." The more information you can obtain before getting to Purchasing will provide you with talking points; talking points based on value and needs you will be helping them with. This is how you prevent your exchange with Purchasing from being all about price.

All of these will help you better understand who is filling each of the roles we covered earlier as you move through the selling process. These will help you steer the conversations toward the desired outcome. They will help you help them.

It is also important to never allow a single person to give you the impression they are your contact for the entire company. The larger the company, the more segmented it tends to be – meaning your contact may have influence over only a small part of the company. If someone tells you they are the only one that needs to be involved you may have found your Road Blocker. Be wary. A single person may be the sole Decision Maker, but unless they are in the C-Suite they probably are not though. Even the C-Suite has to answer to the CEO, who has to answer to the board. Rarely in a large company is it ever a single person.

This is why you must always be prospecting in big companies, regardless of the number of contacts you may already have with them. Think about it – the more contacts you have, the more ways you will be able to help them.

"People deal too much with the negative, with what is wrong. Why not try and see the positive things, to just touch those things and make them bloom?" - Thich Nhat Hanh

I mentioned Optimizers are often eternal optimists; so are salespeople. As such, it is important to understand when to walk away. Earlier in the book we talked about your most valuable asset – your time. Remember you get to choose how and on who you spend it. So, when is enough, enough? When is it better to reallocate your time to someone else? When do you move on to help someone else?

Each situation is unique.

The biggest problem most salespeople have walking away is usually the size of the prize. The huge opportunity that would change your career is something you just don't want to miss. To close this large customer with this huge deal to make your numbers for the next three years. Sounds amazing! I get it. I have chased those types of customers and opportunities before, especially earlier in my career.

You know what else would be amazing? Winning the lottery. It is the same lure of there being a big prize, but when it comes to the lottery most people are well aware of the extremely long odds. So what is the difference?

I am sorry to say, but there is not one. Quit thinking you are going to be the one in 20 million who will get the really big prospect to respond to you. You may very well starve to death waiting for what may never come.

When it simply becomes impossible to get any information out of a contact, or they ignore you totally, or they ghost you completely, it is time to walk away as the only thing you are doing is wasting time you could better spend on working with people who want your help.

Being an optimist is an admirable trait, but you cannot let your optimism overshadow how you use your time.

There is nothing wrong with walking away from a non-responsive contact.

At the same time, do not let self-doubt convince you that you should keep trying to contact them if you know you cannot help them.

Base your decision on the value you place on your time.

And when you decide your time is better spent elsewhere, you send them the breakup e-mail as your final attempt to connect with them.

"I always like to look on the optimistic side of life, but I am realistic enough to know that life is a complex matter." - Walt Disney

What is the breakup e-mail you ask? It is as follows:

Dear Bob,

The last thing we want to do is become a burden. As such, this will be our final attempt regarding (insert how you are trying to help them here) for now. We have (insert your solution here) to help you with (insert what your solution would help them with) and would relish the opportunity to partner with you. Perhaps in the not-too-distant future. We are here and happy to help whenever you have a need. Just let us know when you are ready.

Thank you,

Note you are not closing the door. You are very much leaving it open to contact them again in the future. What this e-mail does is two things.

First, it triggers an emotional response in the receiver. "Do not want to be a burden." "Final attempt." Most people are inclined to respond to this with an apology and an explanation for their lack of a response. No one wants to be the reason behind someone giving up on them. I cannot tell you how many times a contact has gone silent on me and then responded to this e-mail. Does it work every time? No, but it does a lot of the time. And, when they respond with a reason, you can then use that to re-align efforts and expectations around their reason.

The second thing it does is make them feel like they are in control. You have given them the how, the what, and the why and told them when "they" are ready to contact you. At this point, you are no longer a salesperson to them, but rather a resource. A tool in their toolbelt to use at their discretion. Sure, you are going to follow up with them again in the future as you said you would, but in that moment, they will feel great like they have the power. Making them feel this can also result in a response, which again you can use to re-align efforts and expectations. Try it. At this point they are already not responding to you, so you literally have nothing to lose.

"Big thinkers are specialists in creating positive forward-looking, optimistic pictures in their own minds and in the minds of others." - David Schwartz

With all this talk about prospecting, and contacts, and outreach efforts you must keep track of what you are doing. I will introduce the Cookbook to you to help with this, but you really need a good CRM system. As we just talked about when to walk away, we also need to talk about keeping your pipeline tight and accurate. Keeping people on your active contact list despite not having any success is only going to turn your pipeline into a parking lot. It will clog it. Leads and prospects who have not responded are not leads and prospects and as such they do not deserve to be in your pipeline.

I would never tell you to delete these contacts (or anything from your CRM), but these unresponsive contacts are better suited for some type of non-responsive lead list or a marketing drip campaign list. When it comes to the contacts on these lists you still want to e-mail them, but you want to use a different approach. You want to stop trying to turn them into customers and instead turn them into consumers of your information. You stop trying to help them now and instead focus on keeping them informed and aware of who you are and what you do.

With this approach your goal is to help them in a different way. You want to help them by becoming a trusted and valued source of information. I mentioned earlier that most people see and read your e-mails even if they don't respond. If you can provide them with small bits of value and information consistently over time you will turn them into consumers of your information. Once this occurs it is much easier to turn them into customers as they know you are not just trying to sell them something; you are trying to help them.

Provide them with content you feel would benefit them. You can write this content, aggregate from other sources, or use a combination of both. Keep it simple, because you want to make sure reaching out this way doesn't require too much of your time. Keeping it simple also allows the person receiving the message to be able to read and absorb it quickly.

Do not view nurturing this list as a key activity, because it's not. Your time is better spent dealing with prospects who are readily responding to you.

Use your prospecting plan to guide you when you come back to the names on this non-responsive list and begin reaching out again with active prospecting efforts.

The worst thing you can do is to move a name over to the non-responsive list and just leave it there. Doing this says you feel there is a low probability of ever make this contact a customer. If it seemed possible at one time that they could become a customer, it's probably worth trying a few different approaches before giving up entirely.

"Sometimes the bad things that happen in our lives put us directly on the path to the best things that will ever happen to us." - Nicole Reed

Before starting to compile your prospecting plan, please keep in mind a few more things.

You never want to provide your prospect with enough information to make a decision without you. There is a reason they should engage with you rather than going to your website, right? Make sure they understand what that is.

You never want to allow pricing into your discussion during the prospecting phase. If you contact someone and that is one of the first things out of their mouth – run. You just found someone who buys solely on pricing. Unless you have the lowest price in the industry this is a dead-end. Find another contact.

You never forget the most valuable asset you have is your time. There are only 24 hours in a day and 365 days in a year (minus leap year). You and only you get to choose how you spend your time. Spend it wisely as once spent, you cannot get it back no matter what you do.

You never become mesmerized by the contact who claims they want to do business with you right now. As amazing as that would be, most people in business buy for the future, not the present. Meaning they are most likely looking to get set up for a future need. On occasion, a customer will come to you in dire need and in those few cases they may need something right now, but those are few and far between. Qualify these situations to understand which are which and then prioritize your time accordingly. Never let something else get dropped for not understanding the when of your would-be-customer.

You never make contact with a prospect just for the sake of making contact. You must have a plan. You must be able to add value. You must be able to help them. If not, why are you even contacting them in the first place. If you need someone to talk to give your mom another call. I am sure she would appreciate it.

You never forgo the quick sale for the sake of landing the big sale. We are not playing the lottery. We are not letting it all ride on black. The bigger the sale, the longer it will take for it to close. You need the smaller sales before and around the big sales to balance out your numbers.

The big ones will be a few and will come and go. The small ones will be consistent and will allow you to build a solid foundation for your business.

"An individual's self-concept affects every aspect of human behavior. The ability to learn...the capacity to grow and change...the choice of friends, mates, and careers. It is no exaggeration to say that a strong positive self-image is the best possible preparation for success in life." - Joyce Brothers

As the prospecting section of this book concludes, some advice:

Do not try and apply everything at once. You will be far more successful taking one or two key concepts and putting them into play at the highest level possible. After you are doing the first couple of items well, then begin applying another two. The idea is simple – attempting to do everything at once will overwhelm you and lead to inconsistency. You may even feel the need to give up completely.

To conclude the following list details the things top performing salespeople do regularly. As you read the list, keep one thing in mind...

There is nothing on this list you cannot achieve. The only thing holding you back is your self-doubt.

Top salespeople...

- Plan their weeks and work their plans.

- Do not allow e-mail and other routine activities to consume their time or their mental focus.

- Have a prospecting plan they follow without fail.

- Do not allow their time to be wasted by customers/prospects who are not capable of buying.

- Continually learn and look for ways to improve themselves, and in so doing, look to others to gain insight.

- Know the most important asset they have is their own time.

- Treat people in their companies with the same level of respect, communication, and support they provide their best customers.

- Push themselves to a level of standards far surpassing what others would expect of them.

- Focus on goals in everything they do and understand how being goal oriented allows them to remain disciplined.

- Have positive outlooks on themselves and their environments, never passing blame on others, but accepting full responsibility in everything.

It is your move! Are you ready to move to the next level? It is time to put pen to paper and write out your prospecting plan. Once written, put it into action. Course correct as needed but follow the plan you put in place.

Time to make it stick. Use the following action items to compile your prospecting plan.

– Your Infinite Positivity Plan Follow Up Activities –

- Using all of the information from this book, put pen to paper and write out your prospecting plan.

- Once written, put it into action.

- Course correct as needed but follow the plan you put in place.

Still need some help doing this. Do not worry. I will share some example prospecting plans with you to get you going.

"Excuses are the nails used to build a house of failure." - Jim Rohn

Chapter Sixteen

– Infinite Positivity Prospecting Plan Examples –

What follows are a few examples of what a prospecting plan could look like to help you pull all of this together and to put pen to paper as you create yours. Please feel free to use these examples, to use portions or pieces of them, or to create your own from scratch.

We will call this first example "Trigger Momentum Strategy."

First write down your Elevator Pitch and Value Adds – how are you going to help the people you contact as part of this strategy? Make it as detailed as possible.

Next write down your Target Customers – who are the people you will be contacting to help? This could be target industries or companies. If you use industries, you will need to add another step to break the industry down to the specific companies you will help.

Then, do the same with the Targeted Roles – the job titles that will resonate most with your elevator pitch and value adds. Write down all the roles.

Notice how we started high-level based on how you can help and then started narrowing our focus from the universe to specific people? Now that you have your list of target companies and the roles you want to target, spend some time on LinkedIn and/or ZoomInfo to identify specific individuals. You now have your list of people to contact to help. Fantastic!

But you are not there yet. To complete your plan, you need to define the tactics you will use to connect with those individuals. The "Trigger Momentum Strategy" tactics are as follows:

1) Initial Attempt: E-mail with personalized opener (based on role or compliment new technology). Highlight value proposition. Use personalized subject line (role or company).

(Five Business Days Between)

2) Second Attempt: E-mail to ask a specific question about a relevant process or challenge (pique interest) and request a brief meeting (phone call or virtual meeting).

(Five Business Days Between)

3) Third Attempt: E-mail to ask permission to send information (Capabilities Brochure) and request call to discuss further.

(Five Business Days Between)

4) Fourth Attempt: Phone call and follow up e-mail to request a few minutes to chat about solutions to challenges, briefly mention a case study example.

(Five Business Days Between)

5) Fifth Attempt: LinkedIn invite with message sharing value proposition again, and relevant link or Capabilities Brochure.

(Five Business Days Between)

6) Sixth Attempt: E-mail or phone call to ask for referral to correct person. Breakup E-mail. No Response = Follow up monthly. Start process again with new contact at the company until contact is made.

You now have everything you need to move to action and to execute your prospecting plan. You have this! Make it happen!

"You are allowed to be both a masterpiece and a work in progress, simultaneously." – Unknown

Let's do another. We will call this next example "It's Not Luck Strategy."

As we did with the last example, first write down your Elevator Pitch and Value Adds – how you are going to help the people you contact as part of this strategy.

Then write down your Target Customers – the people you will be contacting to help. Target industries or companies. Your choice. Just keep in mind you cannot sell to an industry so if you start there, you need to add a step to get to the specific companies you will help.

Once you have that, you do the same with the Targeted Roles – the job titles that will benefit most from your elevator pitch and value adds. Write them down.

At this point, with your list of target companies and the roles you want to target, spend some time on LinkedIn and/or ZoomInfo identifying specific individuals. Congratulations! You now have your list of people you can help ready to go.

To complete your plan, you define the tactics you will use to connect with those individuals. The "It's Not Luck Strategy" tactics are as follows:

1) Initial Attempt: E-mail Reach Out Highlighting Value Prop and Requesting a Short Call.

(7-10 Business Days Between)

2) Second Attempt: E-mail Reach Out Highlighting Value Prop and Send Information.

(7 Business Days Between)

3) Third Attempt: E-mail Asking If They Received your E-mails.

(5 Business Days Between)

4) Fourth Attempt: Ask for Referral to Right Person.

(7 Business Days Between)

5) Fifth Attempt: Move to New Contact at Company and Repeat. If No Response > Abandon Reaching Out and Reevaluate Contacts/Company

Move to action and execute. You've got this!

"When love and skill work together, expect a masterpiece." - John Ruskin

And a couple more! We will call this next example "Cool Guy Strategy."

You know the drill by now. Start with your Elevator Pitch and Value Adds. Then your Target Customers followed by your Target Roles. Next spend some time on LinkedIn and/or ZoomInfo identifying specific individuals. Well done! Now, you just need your Tactics, then you are ready to rock and roll.

The "Cool Guy Strategy" tactics are as follows:

1) Initial Attempt: Send prospect connection request via LinkedIn (add customized note).

(1 Business Days Between)

2) Second Attempt: Initial e-mail asking about their role/work at company, reason for outreach, intro call request.

(2 Business Days Between)

3) Third Attempt: Second e-mail referring to initial e-mail, asking to send them more info.

(5-7 Business Days Between)

4) Fourth Attempt: Handwritten note with company's Sell Sheet (made by coordinating with Marketing).

(2 Business Days Between)

5) Fifth Attempt: Phone call, then e-mail if no response (refer to mailed content, other outreach attempts).

(5-7 Business Days Between)

6) Sixth Attempt: Final LinkedIn outreach (send custom manufacturing link).

(3-4 Business Days Between)

7) Seventh Attempt: Final outreach, Breakup e-mail referencing persistence is equal to the dedication they can expect in problem-solving for them.

(5 Business Days Between)

8) Close outreach, move on to next prospect and repeat.

This next one we will call "Relentless Persistence Strategy." The "Relentless Persistence Strategy" tactics are as follows:

1) Initial Attempt: Initial E-mail Reach Out Highlighting Value Prop and Requesting a Brief Call.

(5 Business Days Between)

2) Second Attempt: Second E-mail Reach Out Highlighting Value Prop and Asking if it is Okay to Send Information.

(2 Business Days Between)

3) Third Attempt: Handwritten Letter Highlighting Value Prop with Tri-Fold Brochure and Business Card.

(5 Business Days Between)

4) Fourth Attempt: Phone Call and Immediate E-mail to Customer (If VM) Asking if They Received E-mails and Letter.

(5 Business Days Between)

5) Fifth Attempt: Hail Mary LinkedIn Direct Message Sharing Video or Capabilities Flyer – Ask for Referral to Right Person.

6) Move on to New Contact at Facility and Repeat Until All Roles Are Covered – No Response = Add Another Contact.

Hopefully these examples are helping with your understanding and helping get your creative juices flowing. You have a couple more coming.

"Energy and persistence conquer all things." - Benjamin Franklin

Two more examples then you write yours.

At the risk of sounding like a broken record (or am I repeating this on purpose?), you start with your Elevator Pitch and Value Adds. Then your Target Customers followed by your Target Roles. Next spend some time on LinkedIn and/or ZoomInfo identifying specific individuals. Now, you just need your Tactics, then you are ready to execute.

We will call this next example "Heavy Metal Strategy" and the "Heavy Metal Strategy" tactics are as follows:

DAY 1: Send a personalized e-mail to create intrigue. The message should give the context to the outreach and the reason you are contacting the prospect now. Be sure to make the message about them, not you.

DAY 2: Call and leave a voicemail message referencing the e-mail you sent if you are unable to reach the prospect.

DAY 3: Call at a different time of day from the prior attempt, but don't leave a message.

DAY 4: Do not contact the prospect today.

DAY 5: Call and leave a voicemail message referencing the e-mail you sent if you don't reach the prospect live.

Day 6: Forward your original e-mail message and add content to create more intrigue. Again, keep the message content focused on the prospect, not you. Or send a video e-mail if you have access to that technology.

DAY 7: Call at a different time of day and leave a voicemail message if you don't reach the prospect live. In your message, let them know when you will call again. Here is a piece of gold! Send the prospect a calendar invite for that date and time. In most e-mail systems, when you send an invite, it appears in the recipient's calendar whether the invite is accepted or not.

DAY 8: Call at the time you scheduled and leave a voicemail message if you don't reach the prospect live.

DAY 9: Do not contact the prospect today.

DAY 10: Send the prospect a LinkedIn invite and include the same e-mail content as the message you sent on day six.

DAY 11: Call at a different time of day and leave a voicemail message if you don't reach the prospect live that tells them when you will call again. Send them a calendar invite for that time.

DAY 12: Call at the time you scheduled and leave a voicemail message if you don't reach the prospect live.

DAY 13: Do not contact the prospect today.

DAY 14: Call at a different time, but don't leave a message.

DAY 15: Call at a different time of day and leave a voicemail message if you don't reach the prospect live that tells them when you will call again. Send them a calendar invite for that time.

DAY 16: Call at the time you scheduled and leave a voicemail message if you don't reach the prospect live.

This 16-day campaign is aggressive, but keep in mind some salespeople only try to reach their target contact a few times. This would absolutely differentiate you. I also can't take credit for this one as it comes from Lee Salz's book Sell Different! If you haven't read it, I would highly recommend it.

"If everything seems under control, you're not going fast enough." - Mario Andretti

On to the last one. We will call this one "Getting Drippy Strategy." Here are the tactics:

Utilize a drip campaign in which we reach out to share our value adds and to initiate conversations with the defined contacts at each of our target customers.

Phase one of the drip campaign includes weekly outreaches for four weeks straight to each contact.

Outreach efforts will include one outreach per contact per week and will be a combination of phone calls, e-mails, and LinkedIn (i.e., week 1 – e-mail, week 2 – LinkedIn, week 3 – phone call, week 4 – e-mail).

If no response is received after the second outreach a new contact from the target company will be identified and added to the drip campaign to receive the weekly outreach.

If no response is received after the fourth outreach the drip campaign will be slowed to include bi-weekly outreaches for four weeks for each contact (i.e., week 6 – LinkedIn, week 8 – phone call).

If after the two bi-weekly outreaches no response is received, the drip campaign will again be slowed to include monthly outreaches to each contact. These monthly outreaches will carry on indefinitely until the contact responds or success is found with another contact from the same target company (i.e., week 12 – e-mail, week 16 – LinkedIn, and so on).

If a response is received at any time, the drip campaign for that contact/target company will be ceased and focused efforts to help them along the way to turning them into a customer will occur.

There you have it. Six example prospecting plans for you to use as you see fit.

Now it is your turn. Time to put pen to paper. What is your plan going to entail? What will be your masterpiece?

"You have a masterpiece inside you. One unlike any that has ever been created, or ever will be. If you go to your grave without painting your masterpiece, it will not get painted. No one else can paint it. Only you." - Gordon MacKenzie

If you read through these sample prospecting plans and thought they are A LOT, you are right, they are.

But did you know most replies are received between 4-6 touchpoints?

After collecting years' worth of sales data that spans multiple companies, multiple products, different individuals and aggregating that data together it provides a pretty clear picture when it comes to response rates.

After thousands of outreach efforts, the data shows that on average you can expect to see...

- a 1-2% response rate from your initial outreach.

- a 5-6% response rate from your second.

- a 13-14% response rate from your third.

- an 18-19% response rate from your fourth.

- a 16-17% response rate from your fifth.

- a 15-16% response rate from your sixth.

- a 10-11% response rate from your seventh.

- a 6-7% response rate from your eighth.

- a 3-4% response rate from your ninth.

- a 2-3% response rate from your tenth.

- a 1-2% response rate from your eleventh.

- a 1-2% response rate from your twelfth.

- a 1-2% response rate from your thirteenth.

- after that, response rates fall off entirely.

What does this data mean?

It means for those of you "spraying and praying" sending a single message and hoping something will come of it, you are probably going to see a 1-2% response rate.

It means for those of you willing to do the work it takes to earn the trust that comes with getting a response, that you are going to see your most success between your third and seventh outreach attempt.

It also means that are some stubborn contacts that do take a little longer to respond that if you call it quits after eight attempts, you will miss out on them.

Finally, it also shows that at some point, it is in your best interest as the keeper of your time to move on; to find a new contact and to start the process over again.

So are some of these prospecting plans A LOT? You bet they are. But it is important to understand that A LOT is what it takes to arrive at the outcome you want and to earn the responses and business that follows.

Here are a few action items you can do to help ensure what you have read sticks as you put your prospecting plan into action.

– Infinite Positivity Prospecting Plan Examples Follow-Up Activities –

- Get out there and do!

- Help someone. Help lots of people.

- Make a difference.

- Have fun.

- Learn from your mistakes and continually learn and improve.

- Grow.

- Oh and sell something while you are at it.

"In order for you to be the BEST you can be for others, first you must be BEST for yourself." - Jeffrey Gitomer

Chapter Seventeen

− Another Day in the Life of Infinite Positivity −

How about another reminder and example...

You have already seen a few of these, but here is a real-life example of Infinite Positivity in action to show how you can help your customers solve their challenges and transform your relationship from a transactional one, to a strategic partnership.

This case study demonstrates what you should strive to achieve with your customers to help them solve a challenge. Once you do, who do you think they will call next time they find themself faced with a new challenge?

Case Study:

How We Developed a New Product to Help a Biotech Company Keep Up with the Rapidly Growing Cell Culture Industry

Background:

The customer, a biotechnology company who manufactures custom media for pharmaceutical manufactures. The customer also provides a variety of complementary products to be used along with their medias.

Challenge:

This customer uses Cholesterol in one of their medias. Due to the high usage of Cholesterol in COVID vaccines there wasn't enough product in the market to be used for cell culture applications. As a result, the customer began manufacturing their own Cholesterol, but their usage exceeds their production capacity. Given the situation, the customer needed a solution to allow them to continue supplying the cell culture market with this media.

Solution:

We made the decision to utilize existing resources to manufacture the Cholesterol. The supply chain was established. Manufacturing processes established. The product met quality requirements. Samples were manufactured and sent to the customer for evaluation. Upon testing, it was identified that trace metals, specifically copper and chromium exceeded typical ranges. The metals testing was something the customer tested but was not part of the specifications. After learning of this requirement, the manufacturing process was investigated, and it was determined that the higher levels came from the dryer. The process was updated, and additional samples were manufactured. The customer tested the second set of samples, and the trace metal testing data was provided to the customer on the associated Certificate of Analysis (COA). The process change resolved the matter, and the customer confirmed the samples worked for their application. The manufacturing process was scaled to support the customers ongoing and growing needs for the Cholesterol. In doing so, we were able to ensure the customer could continue to support their growth and the growing cell culture industry in turn.

Infinite Positivity in action…again!

"It doesn't take a lot of difference to make a difference." - Sally McGhee

Chapter Eighteen

– Revenue is NOT a Metric –

After all the talk about prospecting, it is time to turn our attention to what comes next in the process. To what you do once your prospecting efforts work, and you find someone you can help.

Before doing so a word from Lee Salz…

"Revenue is a result of the proper activities and behaviors being performed, at the right frequency, by salespeople. There's nothing you can do about revenue, but there's plenty you can do about the activities and behaviors that lead to it."

It is critical that as a salesperson you understand this. Revenue is out of your control. You cannot force a customer to place an order. If revenue is all you are focusing on your customer will sense your intentions and you will lose. Revenue is a lagging indicator and by the time you have it, you either have it or you don't. Meaning, you don't have the ability to course correct to get more of it in real time.

If that sounds negative, it really isn't as it leads me to a truth you need to understand. There are things within the sales process you have complete and total control over. To get to those things you have to look at the beginning of the sales process rather than the end.

This is where your Cookbook comes into play. The Cookbook, or activity plan, outlines the daily activities, the inputs, that need to occur in order to drive to opportunities. Your Cookbook is also the second of three critical processes needed to be successful.

The Cookbook should be considered your road map to success; no tools and no road map puts us at a disadvantage and causes us to play from behind.

While revenue is a lagging indicator and not entirely in our control (the customer holds the majority of this control), your Cookbook is entirely within your control and designed to drive revenue.

It is compiled based on tracking activities from your daily life as a salesperson and is connects those activities to generating NEW business (Opportunities).

When the Cookbook is used together with an established and documented Sales Process (the first of the three critical processes needed to be successful) it will set you up for success in your role.

Your activities are 100% in your control. The number of e-mails you send, the number of calls you make, the number of referrals you request, the number of LinkedIn invites or messages you send, the number of contacts and companies you focus on. These are all things YOU have complete and total control over. By utilizing a Cookbook to track and trend these activities and the outcomes that result from them, you can proactively and strategically drive to the revenue outcomes you want to achieve.

"Attitude drives actions. Actions drive results. Results drive lifestyles." - Jim Rohn

How you ask? With data. That is how. I will walk you through it.

Like the vast majority of salespeople, you probably have a revenue goal. We start with that, but then need to back calculate all the throughout the sales process back to your activities, your inputs. Here is an example of what this could look like:

- Annual Revenue Goal - $1,000,000

- Earned Business Percentage (based on historical sales data) – 50%

In this scenario, if you have an annual revenue goal of a million dollars and your historical sales data shows that you earn on average 50% of the business you quote, this tells us to set yourself up to successfully achieve your revenue goal you need to quote at least $2,000,000 in business (half of $2M is $1M). Let's keep going back.

-Quoted Business - $2,000,000

-Average dollar amount per quote- $100,000

-Opportunity to Quote Conversion Rate (based on historical sales data) – 50%

Diving further into this scenario, with targeting 20 quotes equating to two million dollars, if you know that half of the opportunities you identify ultimately go on to be quoted after you qualify them, then this tells you that to successfully achieve your revenue goal you need to identify and work at least $4,000,000 in opportunities (half of $4M is $2M). Again, let's keep going backwards.

-Opportunities Identified - $4,000,000

-Average dollar amount per opportunity - $200,000

Everything up to this point is based on the stages of your sales process (opportunity > quote > order > revenue > goal). What comes next is where your Cookbook comes into play.

"The biggest reason people don't succeed is that they don't expose themselves to existing information." - Jim Rohn

If set up properly, your Cookbook will allow you to understand how many outbound efforts (calls, e-mails, referrals, etc.) are necessary to generate an opportunity. While it does require some administrative work to track your activities, doing so will help you to determine how to drive your sales.

If after tracking and trending your activities you are able to determine that on average for every 15 outreach efforts sent/made, you generate one opportunity, then you can use these numbers to drive your success. Based on these sample numbers, if you want to identify $4,000,000 worth of opportunities and your average opportunity value is $200,000, then you need to identify 20 opportunities and earn business from five to meet your sales goal ($1M – 25% earn rate). If it requires 15 outreach efforts to identify a single opportunity, this means you will need to make 300 outreach efforts (20 opportunities x 15 outreach efforts to generate one quote with a 25% or 50% earn rate).

Please note we are talking about averages with all of this, so this formula isn't perfect. It will however put you in the ballpark based on your targets. It is also important that you keep an eye on your numbers, preferably looking at them at least weekly to make sure there are no shifts. If there is a shift in your numbers, by checking them at least weekly it will allow you to course correct in real time. Thus, allowing you to know the score of the game while you are playing it rather than waiting to the end of the game to know how you did.

A bonus of the Cookbook, if set up correctly, it will also help you make your process and messaging more efficient. For example, you may find that your e-mail outreach efforts only generate a 20% response rate while your phone calls generate a 60% response rate. You can use data like this to your advantage. You can use this date to look at the messaging of your e-mails to see what changes you can make to improve that response rate. You can also use it to ensure you are spending more time on the phone than you are sending e-mails as that is a more efficient means for you to connect with your customers and to generate opportunities.

Let's put all of this together…

- Annual Revenue Goal - $1,000,000

- Earned Business Percentage (based on historical sales data) – 50%

- Quoted Business - $2,000,000

- Average dollar amount per quote- $100,000

- Number of quotes - 20

- Opportunity to Quote Conversion Rate (based on historical sales data) – 50%

- Opportunities Identified - $4,000,000

- Average dollar amount per opportunity - $200,000

- Number of opportunities - 20

- Outreach efforts – 300

These are simple numbers to demonstrate the process, but this formula works for all numbers.

In addition to tracking and trending these, you should also consider tracking your sales cycle – the number of days from when an opportunity is identified to when you earn the business. This will allow you to understand at what point in the year you stop playing for the current year and begin playing for next year. For example, if you have a 90-day sales cycle that means anything you start working on in October, November, and December most likely won't come to conclusion until the start of the next year. That shows that you are really working October to September, rather than from January through December. Knowing this is vital to scheduling your efforts accordingly.

To repeat Lee again, "Revenue is a result of the proper activities and behaviors being performed, at the right frequency, by salespeople. There's nothing you can do about revenue, but there's plenty you can do about the activities and behaviors that lead to it." By understanding your process, your data, and your activities you take complete control over the inputs to your process and these inputs are what drive the outcomes. These input, your activities, are 100% in your control. Use them to your advantage. You have this!

Pictured below is a sample Cookbook you can use:

If you are interested in receiving an editable version of this Cookbook, I am more than happy to provide you with a ready to use version. You simply need to update the dates in it and then begin tracking. Easy. Just contact me and I will send it to you.

You may have noticed that I mentioned three critical processes needed to be successful in sales, but I only mentioned two. If you haven't already assumed or guessed, the third critical process to be successful is this an overall approach and philosophy such as Infinite Positivity.

"Perhaps happiness is always to be found in the journey uphill, and not in the fleeting sense of satisfaction awaiting at the next peak." - Jordan Peterson

Chapter Nineteen

– Managing Questions –

Infinite Positivity has nothing to do with the product, service, or technology you are selling, and everything to do with the ways you sell.

Nothing says you have to change everything in order to make significant gains/improvement. All you need is incremental improvement to make a BIG difference. Consider the following example:

	Current	5% More	10% More	15% More
Opportunities	100	105	110	115
Average Opp. $$$	$20,000	$20,000	$20,000	$20,000
Opp. to Quote Conversion Rate	80%	80%	80%	80%
Quotes	80	84	88	92
Quote to Win Conversion Rate	50%	50%	50%	50%
Wins	40	42	44	46
Revenue	$800,000	$840,000	$880,000	$920,000

By doing 10% more, based on this model you would be able to add $80K in additional sales. Infinite Positivity is about finding ways to differentiate yourself by helping people to obtain incremental improvements that make a BIG impact.

After your prospecting efforts have succeeded and you begin talking with a potential customer, one of the best and first place you can achieve this incremental improvement is how you manage your customer's questions. I intentionally used "manage" as that is exactly what you need to do.

Have you ever heard the old saying, "an ounce of prevention is worth a pound of cure." This typically refers to a person's health, encouraging people to eat well and exercise rather than face health challenges later. It might also be used when talking about how a person manages their finances rather than them getting buried under a mountain of debt. In the Infinite Positivity context it refers to managing customer questions.

Think about this. What if you could prevent opportunities from getting stuck? What if you were able to eliminate confusion from the process to keep things simple for you and your customer? What if you were able to provide yourself with a tool to help you earn more business? Wouldn't you want that?

"The uncreative mind can spot wrong answers, but it takes a creative mind to spot wrong questions." - Antony Jay

For example, if you know more than half the people you are trying to help have the same questions, why would you ever let those questions come up? By letting routine questions come up, you then have to respond to them. "Respond" isn't proactive, intentional, or strategic. It is the opposite – it is reactive and defensive. At that point, your opportunity is at risk, and you find yourself fighting to get it back on track. Why would you put yourself in this position? Why would you let yourself lose control of the opportunity? Those who ask the questions control the conversation. When all you are doing is answering questions in a reactive manner, your customer is in control, not you. Preemptively address these questions – if it comes up a lot you should already have a good answer.

If that is not enough, by simply responding you miss out on an opportunity to differentiate yourself; to be more than just another salesperson. There is no way to eliminate your customer's questions, nor should you want to as if they are not participating in the conversation or showing interest in what you offer, you are probably trying to help the wrong person. What we are talking about is how to get ahead of these questions so you can use the answers to guide the customer through the process. To do so you need to ask yourself what are the common questions my customers ask. You have heard them all. If you think hard enough you know what they are.

It does not matter what you offer – the same questions come up time and time again.

The most common one probably has to do with price. How much is it? Can I get a quote? What is this going to cost me?

The challenge you face with this question is customers usually ask it prematurely, often times before you have even determined how best to help them. Given this is something on everyone's mind and a question we all get asked you would assume it is vital to earning the business, right? Wrong.

Lee Salz summed it up best in his book Sell Different! Where he points out if price is the be-all, end-all decision factor, then we would all:

- Wear all the cheapest clothes. No more Gucci, Prada, or Fendi. Just inexpensive materials.

- Eat the cheapest food. No more foodies. Just food for basic nutritional purposes.

- Have the cheapest phones. No more iPhone in your pocket. Might as well go back to the days when phones were just phones.

- Drive the cheapest cars. No more luxury brands, no more muscle cars, and no more fancy EVs. Just something practical.

- Live in the cheapest houses. Simple gray boxes designed for shelter only.

- Use the cheapest toilet paper. No more ultra soft 2-ply for you. You might as well use a newspaper.

- Sit in the worst seats at the ball game. Who wants to sit courtside? It is a much better experience to have to squint to make out who the players are.

- Shave with a single blade razor. As someone with a shaved head, sorry, but no.

But people don't do these things. Do you? Remember, many people have bought from your company. It probably was not all due to price. It was the meaningful value the customer obtained from your process, your product, your service, etc.

Price is not the end-all, be-all. It is a conversation point along the way. A potentially dangerous conversation point.

"Do not pay too much attention to fame, power, or money. Some day you will meet a person who cares for none of these, and then you will know how poor you are." - Rudyard Kipling

I say this as if you answer the question, you lose. The conversation with the customer becomes laser focused on price as it was introduced into the process too early before value was established. Unless what you sell is the cheapest on the market, sharing the price prematurely is most likely going to put the opportunity in jeopardy.

But, if you refuse to answer the question, you also lose. The customer will become irritated you will not answer their question and the conversation will take on a negative tone, which can make for a very short call or meeting.

Rock meets hard place. You are stuck. You only have two choices when this question comes up too early in the process - tell them or not tell them - and both lead to a high likelihood of not moving forward.

So, what are you supposed to do? You use a third option. You know it is going to come up, so rather than wait for it and hope it does not, you embrace it and proactively set the stage for the right time to share the information.

As an example, let's look at the services of a financial adviser. As is the case for most industries, advisors in this industry know one of the first questions they will get is about pricing. For them it comes in the form of "a request for their rate." Think about it though. If they share their rate, the person hangs up and calls another adviser to shop for a lower price. If they refuse to tell them the rate, the potential customer will hang up the phone angry and never call back. It's a lose-lose proposition.

On top of that, there really isn't an answer to that question as there are many different financial services they could provide, each of which has a different rate associated with it. Plus, most advisers know the majority of their customers come to them because they lack the level of financial expertise that they do meaning they may not know the services they need. Without being able to advise their customers on their given situation, what are they to do?

They do not let the price question get in their way by addressing it before it is even asked. They manage the conversation as follows.

"If you don't go after what you want, you'll never have it. If you don't ask, the answer is always no. If you don't step forward, you're always in the same place." - Nora Roberts

"I know a big question on your mind is what is your rate? That question would be on my mind too. There are many different financial services, each with different end goals. Selecting someone to help you with your finances is a big decision for you and you want to make sure you make an informed decision. If we can have a ten- to fifteen-minute conversation, this will help us identify the right services for what you want to accomplish and then I can then share the rate for it."

This approach accomplishes several objectives for them. First, it leans into the question by proactively bringing it up before the customer does. Second, it demonstrates they understood their customers and how they are most likely feeling at that moment when they talked about it being a big decision and the importance of finding the right services to accomplish what they want to accomplish. Third, it demonstrates expertise by talking about the different services, each with different end goals. Finally, it further differentiates themself from others who would share a random rate to avoid the possibility of upsetting the customer.

This approach provides several benefits, some of which were just mentioned but deserve repeating. By doing this...

- You proactively addressed the price before it came up.

- You demonstrated you understand your customer and appreciate an important question of theirs.

- You explained that providing a price is not as simple as tossing out a number.

- You allowed the customer to feel they are still in control by asking permission to provide pricing later, but you are really the one in control.

- You differentiated yourself from the competition through how you sell.

This approach isn't just designed to get out ahead of pricing questions. It can be and should be used to proactively address other potential questions as well.

This approach should be used when there is no answer to the question.

Not to beat the pricing question to death, but it is the most common, so another example, if you cannot compete on price, why wait for it to become a question once you provide it to the customer? Instead, proactively come up with something to differentiate you and your products/services and share it as part of the conversations you have with your customer early in the process. You could say something like:

"You should probably know we are not usually the lowest price for this. Yet, we have over a thousand customers who see the value in what we have to offer. Today, I'll share with you some of the differences our customers appreciate, and you can decide if those differences are meaningful to you."

Rather than have an approach based on crossing your fingers hoping that the customer is not familiar with prices for what they are wanting to buy, you have instead proactively positioned that there is value in what you have to offer. Based on your statement regarding your number of customers, it communicates that others have perceived meaningful value and bought from your company. And you leave the determination of what is most meaningful to them based on the value you will share.

"Being humble means recognizing that we are not on earth to see how important we can become, but to see how much difference we can make in the lives of others." - Gordon B. Hinckley

Hopefully you are beginning to understand the power of proactively answering questions. This approach should be used to turning a shortcoming into a positive.

If you know your customers are concerned with your size, your location, or some other aspect of your company, don't bury your head in the sand and hope the topic does not come up. Instead create a positive story that uses your shortcomings to differentiate yourself from the competition that leads the customer to want to do business with you.

Want an example? In the life science industry it is common to maintain confidentiality agreements with each of your customers -- and "confidentiality" is a strong differentiator. Those agreements even prohibit the sharing of the names of the companies you work with. Confidentiality can be a great benefit to protect the highly sensitive lifesaving and life-enhancing products these life science companies develop. They appreciate confidentiality, but this can be a question of concern.

At some point in conversations, in the life science industry you are still going to be asked to share some of the companies you work with as a means of gauging your worthiness. Yes, even despite their own desires and requirements around confidentiality. If you answer the question, you satisfy the worthiness questions, but you violate the confidentiality provisions of your contract(s) with other customers that can put you at risk losing them or worse yet, being sued. If they don't answer the question, you don't pass the worthiness test which can result in the conversation becoming negative. Either way, again, it is a lose-lose situation.

Consider a third option - what if instead you used an approach to proactively address the confidentiality question early in the initial discussions to ensure the question does not result in a lose-lose situation. Perhaps you tell them:

"A question probably on your mind is who are we supporting? I'd be wondering that as well. One of the aspects that our customers appreciate about our company is confidentiality, given the sensitive nature of what companies like yours do and the help we provide them. When we work with a customer, we never share their names. You would also have that same benefit which reduces your risk and protects your business by working with us."

Similar to the price question, you demonstrate an understanding of the customer, while showing your expertise in their industry, all while positioning a meaningful differentiator. If you wait for them to ask who your customers are, you lose the opportunity to do this. By proactively addressing concerns, you can demonstrate expertise as you show you understand what is on their mind. As you communicate your concern for their risk and to protect their business you create meaningful differentiation in how you sell.

"When you approach a problem, strip yourself of preconceived opinions and prejudice, assemble and learn the facts of the situation, make the decision which seems to you to be the most honest, and then stick to it." - Chester Bowles

To best help your customers it is important to hone both your listening and your questioning skills, so you can dig deep into a customer's questions to uncover real opportunities to help them, as well as your abilities to proactively get ahead of these questions to best manage the conversation.

Hopefully you are in agreement with the need to proactively and intentionally address these questions, but maybe you still aren't sure how to do so. Do not worry. I am going to help you. What follows is the result of an exercise I completed with a team I manages that surfaced the best practices for proactively and intentionally address the ten most common questions that come up throughout the sales process, as well as the process to best address them.

The tables that follow detail these ten most common questions, when they are most likely to come up, why they come up, when it is best to address them, and what to ask, say, or do to resolve them. Enjoy!

"If you are not moving closer to what you want in life, you probably aren't doing enough asking." - Jack Canfield

Most common sales obstacles and how to resolve them. Let's get into those now:

Question - How much is it?

When is this likely to come up (Prospecting, Discovery, Solution Development, Contracting)? - Usually during Prospecting and Discovery.

Why does it come up? – It is a burning question on everyone's mind as everything costs something. It could also be a check in the box for an RFQ/RFP, or because of a three-quote requirement. It may also come up due to an issue or immediate need.

When it is best to address it (before it comes up or after)? - Both

What should you say, ask, and do to address it? - You can say, "I know a big question on your mind is price. That question would be on my mind too. As you might imagine, there are several factors that affect pricing for what we offer. If I can ask you a few questions, that will allow me to provide the right pricing for you. Is that okay?" Or you can tell them, "We view our customers as partners and until we establish a level of trust and transparency based on an understanding of your needs, it's premature to provide pricing. May I ask you a few questions so we can obtain that understanding?"

How about another question?

Question - I've never heard of your company.

When is this likely to come up (Prospecting, Discovery, Solution Development, Contracting)? - Typically, during prospecting, at trade shows, when adding new contacts to the conversation during discovery.

Why does it come up? - Due to low representation in the market and/or as a result of you expanding your capabilities. It could also occur if the individuals don't want to be sold to or if they had a bad experience with another supplier.

When it is best to address it (before it comes up or after)? - Both

What should you say, ask, and do to address it? - Tell them, "If you can tell me about your role/your company/what you are working on, I will walk you through who we are based on how we could help you with what is specifically on your plate. Would that be possible?" Or you could say, "Considering we are talking; I assume you have a challenge you are looking for help resolving. If you can help me understand that I can walk you through what we do and how we can help you solve your problem. Would that be possible?"

"Believe in yourself and all that you are. Know that there is something inside you that is greater than any obstacle." - Christian D. Larson

Question - Your price is too high.

When is this likely to come up (Prospecting, Discovery, Solution Development, Contracting)? - Discovery, solution development, contracting, and when earning the order.

Why does it come up? - The customer does not see or understand the value you offer based on price - the value to price correlation may not be obtainable. You may also be talking with the wrong person.

When it is best to address it (before it comes up or after)? - Both, but ideally before it arises.

What should you say, ask, and do to address it? - You can tell them, "Rarely are we the low-cost provider, but if we are able to understand your objectives/initiatives/goals and/or your company's top priorities, through understanding that, we can help you to build a pricing model to align our pricing and justify any differences. Could we walk you through that process?" You can also use information you obtained during qualification (waste reduction, yield, quality, etc.) the customer shared was important to articulate value and remind them of the value that goes into the pricing.

What other questions typically come up?

Question - We are concerned about your size.

When is this likely to come up (Prospecting, Discovery, Solution Development, Contracting)? - Discovery, solution development, contracting, and when earning the order.

Why does it come up? - The customer perceives risk/stability/ability to perform, or they had a bad experience with another smaller company.

When it is best to address it (before it comes up or after)? - Both.

What should you say, ask, and do to address it? - You can say, "I completely understand. Big companies do what they do well, but outside of that they usually are not nimble and flexible enough to help with the niche needs to quickly solve the ever-expanding market's problems. We pride ourselves on our size, as it allows us to drive to personalized solutions that truly help our customers."

Hopefully you are seeing how we are proactively and intentionally addressing these questions to manage the conversation.

"I think a hero is an ordinary individual who finds strength to persevere and endure in spite of overwhelming obstacles." - Christopher Reeve

Hopefully you are starting to understand the power of proactively answering questions. This approach should be used to turn shortcomings into positives. Let's do another.

Question - This is not a priority right now.

When is this likely to come up (Prospecting, Discovery, Solution Development, Contracting)? - During solution development, contracting, and when earning the order.

Why does it come up? - Priorities shift in a world of consistently fighting fires. It could also come from a lack of understanding of the timeline, or from a lack of demonstrated value. It could also be due to your urgency (time to source/set up accounts/late) which could lead to you missing the window of opportunity.

When it is best to address it (before it comes up or after)? - When it comes up.

What should you say, ask, and do to address it? - You can tell them, "I am sure you have a million and a half things on your plate, so can you help me understand on a scale of 1-10 how high of a priority you would rank this based on everything else on your plate right now?" Or maybe, "Understood; what are your priorities right now? Maybe we can help with them and then come back to this later?" You could also say, "When we spoke earlier in this process you shared (using information obtained from discovery/qualification), is this no longer the case?"

Another!

Question - I do not have the authority to make this decision.

When is this likely to come up (Prospecting, Discovery, Solution Development, Contracting)? - Typically, during discovery and solution development. Hopefully not later in the process than that.

Why does it come up? - You are talking to the wrong person. Or maybe they need to evaluate samples or obtain some type of approval from Quality Assurance (QA) or from their boss. They may also need to go through a change control or a consensus buying process.

When it is best to address it (before it comes up or after)? - Both (ideally before it arises).

What should you say, ask, and do to address it? - There are a few for this one. Let's rattle them off. "If we can demonstrate value to you for our solution, would you be willing to introduce me to who can make the decision?" "How can we help you to present this to your boss so you and your team can take advantage of our solution?" "Who is on the change control committee, so we can ensure we address the needs of each member?" "What would your sample evaluation entail, how long will it take, and what would you consider a successful evaluation to look like?" "What does your approval process entail and how can we help you to move this through that process?" "Are there other matters/issues you do have approval for?"

A few more to go.

"Crystalize your goals. Make a plan for achieving them and set yourself a deadline. Then, with supreme confidence, determination, and disregard for obstacles and other people's criticisms carry out your plan." - Paul Meyer

Question - We want to conduct a pilot (test a sample) before agreeing to a full charge or moving forward.

When is this likely to come up (Prospecting, Discovery, Solution Development, Contracting)? - Prospecting, discovery, solution develop, contracting, and when earning the order.

Why does it come up? - It's may be part of their supplier qualification for critical raw materials. This may be to validate or re-validate (side by side comparison). It could be for risk mitigation when making a change. It could also be a requirement for custom manufactured products, biologics, diagnostic test kits, or other highly regulated products.

When it is best to address it (before it comes up or after)? - Before it arises for custom/bulk products, or when it arises for off-the-shelf products.

What should you say, ask, and do to address it? - For custom/bulk you tell them, "What does your evaluation process entail, how long does it take, and what criteria would you be looking for to consider the evaluation successful? We would also need to understand your annual consumption to ensure we can support you and that we can scale with you as needed." For off-the-shelf you tell them, "Please purchase what you need for your evaluation; if it doesn't work, we will work with you to return the material/offer a refund/troubleshoot/provide an alternative. We are that confident in our products and our ability to help you."

Remember, Infinite Positivity has nothing to do with the product, service, or technology you are selling, and everything to do with the ways you sell. Here is another one.

Question - We must buy through an RFP/RFQ.

When is this likely to come up (Prospecting, Discovery, Solution Development, Contracting)? - Contracting and when earning the order.

Why does it come up? - This is simply how some companies buy based on policies and the dollar amount of the purchase. They may also be looking to consolidate supply chain/vendors (multiple products at once). Or they could be doing some type of federally funded grant research where this is required by law (over $10K).

When it is best to address it (before it comes up or after)? - Both.

What should you say, ask, and do to address it? - Try saying, "We want to help you get exactly what you need. The more information we have, the better we can support you. As such, can you please walk us through what your buying process from here through making a decision and purchasing will entail, so we can best align our efforts and expectations?"

Just a couple more now.

"You are only confined by the walls you build yourself." - Andrew Murphy

Just two more of the most common questions that come up during the sales process. What are they you ask?

Question - I'm concerned about the ramifications of your solution not working properly.

When is this likely to come up (Prospecting, Discovery, Solution Development, Contracting)? – Usually during solution development, when earning the order, or during contracting.

Why does it come up? – Because they had a bad experience with a previous vendor, or a bad prior experience with you. They may also be getting cold feet, or they may not be fully convinced by the value adds. This stems from a lack of trust and/or concern for their own personal welfare – if your solution does not work, they are the one who made the decision to proceed.

When it is best to address it (before it comes up or after)? – Both, but ideally before it arises. It's best discussed over the phone/video/in person to give them confidence and demonstrate your commitment to them.

What should you say, ask, and do to address it? – Ask them, "What specifically about the solution are you concerned with?" Or you can tell them, "If you can help me understand your concerns, we would be more than happy to address them. In fact, we would suggest we schedule a call with you and your team, so we can walk you ALL through how this will best align with your needs together. Would that be possible?" You could also say, "Understood. We stand behind our products 100% and should anything go wrong, you will have our full support as we work with you to make it right."

And finally...

Question - We don't want to change our process to change providers.

When is this likely to come up (Prospecting, Discovery, Solution Development, Contracting)? – Early, during prospecting, discovery, or solution development.

Why does it come up? – Because of perceived difficulties in making a change. This could be due to them being single sourced, or a result of their overly bureaucratic processes, or a result of validations or change control. Difficulties lead to it being hard and most people will do what they can to avoid hard work.

When it is best to address it (before it comes up or after)? – Before it arises. You want to get out ahead of this one.

What should you say, ask, and do to address it? – In an early conversation say, "We understand making changes in regulated environments isn't always easy, but we've been able to help companies like yours to set up a secondary supplier to reduce their overall risk and to provide a safety net for your supply chain. Would you be open to learning about how we could do this for you?" If that does not work try asking, "What would making this change entail on your end? Once we understand that, we can detail out each step of this process so we can help you with your processes to make this as simple as possible."

And there you have it. Using this proactive approach to managing your customer conversations isn't complicated, but it can make the difference between being able to actually help your customer, or them never giving you the chance. The choice seems simple.

"Three choices in life: give up, give in, or give it your all." - Dwayne "The Rock" Johnson

Chapter Twenty

– And then there was Infinite Positivity –

A final reminder and an example before we wrap up Infinite Positivity for now...

This will be a quick break to focus on a real-life example of Infinite Positivity in action. To show you how you can help your customers solve their challenges and by doing so, transform your relationship with them from a transactional one to a strategic partnership.

This case study demonstrates what you can achieve with your customers as you help them solve a challenge. Keep in mind doing so also sets you up for future success as who do you think they will call next time they find themself with a new challenge?

Case Study:

How we created a one-of-a-kind solution to extend stability and increase consistency for peracetic acid lots.

Background:

When a customer who was buying peracetic acid from a well-known life science catalog company approached us with two major problems, our chemists and engineers worked together to create a completely personalized, one-of-a-kind solution. We were able to take a labor-intensive, frustrating process—aliquoting peracetic acid every three weeks, as well as dealing with lot inconsistency and degradation—and:

- Right size the volume to negate the need for aliquoting (from 100mL down to 11mL),

- Extend stability (shelf life from 4-5 weeks to 7 months), and

- Increase consistency (from a 13% range down to 2%).

During one of our visits to this customer's facility, they shared with us that they were utilizing a 39% peracetic acid that they were purchasing from a well-known life science catalog company. The customer had to purchase it in 100mL containers every three weeks, and then would aliquot it down to 8mL and 11mL quantities. They did this for two reasons. First, those volumes were what aligned with their process and how they used the acid, but they were not commercially available. Second, and more problematic, peracetic acid is both light sensitive (photosensitive) and oxygen sensitive. The acid was therefore degrading rapidly in the 100mL container that it arrived in.

Challenge:

At the time we learned about this problem, the customer's solution was to aliquot the acid into brown HDPE 60mL plastic bottles, vacuum seal them into a pouch, and store them in the refrigerator until use. However, despite going through this inconvenient and expensive process, the acid was still experiencing rapid degradation after just a couple weeks in the brown HDPE bottles. That wasn't the final problem, either. Although the acid this customer was purchasing from the catalog company was labeled with a concentration of 39%, the Certificate of Analysis (COA) they received with it listed the concentration as a range from 25%-38%. This large range meant there were inconsistencies with each lot they received.

"Each person must live their life as a model for others." - Rosa Parks

Solution:

Our team of chemists and engineers put our heads together to address the issues this customer was experiencing. The first and easiest problem to solve was right sizing their volume. As a chemical manufacturer, we manufactured the solution and custom filled it in both 8mL and 11mL volumes. This eliminated the need for the customer to aliquot it. The acid would simply show up ready to use.

The second, and more challenging, problem was to extend the stability of the acid and bring consistency to the lots. This would require a process quite different from our normal processes, which was the first complication. We needed to address the photosensitivity, which we could do by utilizing the brown HDPE bottles, but we would need to take this a step further, so we could also address the sensitivity to oxygen.

Addressing the oxygen sensitivity would require two things. First, we would have to reduce the headspace in the bottle, and second, we would have to change the environment within the bottle to not only be free of oxygen, but to remain that way for a prolonged period. To accomplish this, we set up a process in which we filled 11mL of the 39% Peracetic Acid into 15mL bottles, so the reduced head space would help with the stability of the acid. We also include a nitrogen blanket to replace the oxygen that would otherwise be in the bottle—this is also to help with the product's stability. Once sealed, the bottles were placed individually into foil pouches. A vacuum was pulled on the pouches to remove any further oxygen, and the pouches were finally heat sealed. This locked the acid in an oxygen-free environment. We also refrigerated the final bottles at 2-8°C to further extend the stability.

Although nitrogen blanketing, a process in which you replace oxygen with nitrogen, is a simple practice widely used in the chemical, pharmaceutical, food processing, and petroleum refining industries, its potential to improve productivity, stability, and safety is often overlooked. In this case, it was exactly what this acid needed.

"To improve is to change; to be perfect is to change often." - Winston Churchill

Now, we had just one last problem to solve: lot consistency. We had right sized the volume to their actual usage and process. We had completely altered the environment the acid was exposed to extend the stability. The final step was establishing an analytical concentration test as part of the lot release criteria, which our Quality team was able to do.

We presented all of this to the customer as a solution and they decided to proceed and after five months we manufactured the first lot in August. Based on the 39% Peracetic Acid they were using before and its stability, this lot would have degraded beyond usability in just one month, by September. As part of a stability study we also performed to verify the stability of the acid, we tested the concentration in March, seven months after it was manufactured, and the concentration was still in line with its original values at the time of manufacturing.

We were able to put a lot of checks in the boxes for this customer with this challenge. Shortly thereafter, they continued to bring project after project to us, and they quickly grew from a small customer to one of our biggest.

That is the power of Infinite Positivity.

"We don't receive wisdom; we must discover it for ourselves after a journey that no one can spare us." - Marcel Proust

Chapter Twenty-one

– Not a Great Salesperson –

Early in my career the owner of a company I was working for sat me down and told me I was not a great salesperson, but I was going to make one hell of a sales manager. I was completely taken aback by his comment and immediately got ready to fight. At the time I joined the company a year earlier and had hands down earned the most revenue and new business since joining. I am very analytical, so I was prepared to start producing my numbers and various successes, when I realized there was a second part of his comment. It took me a minute to realize the backward complement was in fact a complement and in that moment, he went on to explain that he was promoting me into a sales director role – my first sales leadership role actually. While I was thrilled, excited, and nervous about the promotion, I couldn't get over his comment. It irked me to no end.

As I moved into the new role, I inherited the existing sales team that I had been part of for the previous year, and I started trying to figure out what I was doing. I have always been confident in my abilities and had the results to back them up, but I was only responsible for me and my revenue goals. I never thought about how I did it. My new role pushed me to figure it out so I could help the team I had at the time grow the business. Sure there were bumps in the road along the way, but with time, I began to extract the method to my madness from what I was doing and put it on paper in a document I came to call the Strategic Business Development Manual. The more I was able to get my thoughts and concepts out of my head into the manual the better I could prepare, mentor, and train the team I was responsible for to meet our growth goals.

I also started a habit of buying each member of my team a book each quarter. The topic was focused on something our team could learn and improve upon. Everyone would read the book and then we would come together as a team to discuss the many lessons learned and the key takeaways. This amplified the learning as we are all in different places and experiencing different things at any given time, so something that resonated with one member of the team could have been completely overlooked by another. But, when these lessons learned and key takeaways are shared and discussed, it allows everyone to benefit from that same resonation. These discussions were documented and added to the manual.

I also had a rule that I shared with the team and have already shared it in this book, that you have to take at least one thing from the reading and implement it into your daily life. Ideally more than one thing, but at least one.

"The goal is not to be perfect by the end. The goal is to be better today." - Simon Sinek

For most of my adult life, not so much when I was younger, I have been obsessed with continued education and learning. I also have a deep appreciation for business and self-help books. Because of this, I set a goal for myself to read 24 business and/or self-help books each and every year. Minus a couple wabbles, I have consistently done this for the last decade. Not a surprise, but my lessons learned and key takeaways from those books were also added to the manual. So too was content from various sales trainings and programs I underwent.

I also became a meticulous note taker, particularly due to the highly regulated industry I worked in but also as a way to capture and learn from my experiences. You have read quite a few case studies throughout this book, all of them came from my personal experiences as I helped various customers. And yes, those experiences were added to the manual.

The manual has continually evolved over the course of many years, and it picked up content from numerous sources, and spanned experiences from multiple companies where I was able to work with amazing teams of people and with customers changing the world. I was and continue to be fortunate to have been able to learn from all these people and from all the experiences I encountered along the way.

I did not realize it, nor did I ever imagine in my wildest dreams, when I started the manual all those years ago that it would turn into what it did. That it would eventually become Infinite Positivity.

"Doing what you did yesterday will always get you to today. You have to do things differently in order to get to tomorrow." - Aaron Schieving

I would be remiss if I didn't go back to the comment that started all of this that I wasn't a great salesperson, but I was going to make one hell of a sales manager. I have a framed quote on my desk from the beloved rapper Busta Rhymes that reads, "if you aren't going to be part of the greatest, you have to be the greatest yourself." It has been there for years. As someone who looks at that quote every day, I am sure you can imagine how I felt being told I wasn't great. While it wasn't the owner's intent, it did spur me on to continue to earn business by helping my customers at an even greater rate than before, all while building and learning to lead a team, among many other things.

It wasn't until after many successful years had passed that it finally occurred to me, and I was able to make my own sense of that comment. Turns out he was right. I am not a great salesperson. That is because I do not actually sell. You are at the end of the book at this point, so think about it after everything you have read, and you will understand this is true as well. I don't sell people - I help them.

I can honestly say, I do not go into conversations with customers thinking about numbers or revenue. Those things are usually the last thing on my mind during those interactions. I can even be quoted telling people on the teams I was responsible for that I don't care about revenue, or quotes, or dollars. I can say this after living the Infinite Positivity model my entire life.

I am fortunate to have been able to help a lot of people over the years and in doing so have demonstrated that I am a person they can count on when in need. By helping them and earning their trust and appreciation, those customers followed me throughout my career, from company to company. It has been something remarkable that I am incredible grateful for.

I actually had a member of my team ask me one time how I got all the opportunities I did. I told her I would let her in on my secret, but only if she told everyone. I then told her right now, to get these opportunities, I did absolutely nothing. She looked at me bewildered. I went on to tell her they came as a result of how I helped these customers in the past, some many years ago, some last year, some just last month or week.

With Infinite Positivity the business will come, but your impact will be forever.

"It's not so important what people think when you come in, it's what people think when you leave." - Jurgen Klopp

Living the Infinite Positivity model has led me to a career I am truly proud of that has allowed me to provide for my family all while having a significant impact on the people I work with. I have trained many amazing individuals using the Strategic Business Development Manual on how to achieve this themselves. And, I have been fortunate to see most of them benefit from it and actually achieve the same. Now, I am hopeful that Infinite Positivity does the same for you.

A parting and important thought with all of this. As I shared, I am obsessed with continued education and learning. I am also me and you are you. We are not the same. And that is important to note as while I hope Infinite Positivity provides a path you can follow, exactly how you follow it is completely up to you.

There is a saying that no man ever steps in the same river twice, for it is not the same river, and he is not the same man. We are constantly being influenced by the world around us. Everything and everyone we come in contact with has an impact on us. As such, you are not the same person from day to day. You yourself are constantly learning and evolving. The river is ever flowing and ever changing. The river is what you are exposed to. Sometimes it is full and wide. Other times it dries out to a mere trickle. Based on all of this, it is up to you to do what you will with this book.

If you enjoyed reading it and that is merely it, the impact will be minimal. On the other hand, if you take and implement the lessons learned into your daily life, the impact will be greater. You get to choose the person you are by controlling the flow of your river. The choice is yours to make it positive.

Now get out there and do!

"Nice guys appear to finish last, but usually they are running in a different race." - Ken Blanchard and Norman Vincent Peale

Here are a few books that will supplement what you have read and that will help you on your journey to Infinite Positivity. These have all positively influenced me and I wanted to share them with you. I would highly recommend them all. Happy reading!

- Up your Game by David Bradford

- Nine Lies About Work by Marcus Buckingham and Ashley Goodall

- The Jolt Effect by Matthew Dixon and Ted McKenna

- The Little Gold Book of Positive Attitude by Jeffrey Gitomer

- Selling Boldly by Alex Goldfayn

- A Mind for Sales by Mark Hunter

- High-Profit Prospecting by Mark Hunter

- Momentum by Shama Hyder

- Gap Selling by Keenan

- Be Our Guest by Theodore Kinni

- The Advantage by Patrick Lencioni

- 6 Types of Working Genius by Patrick Lencioni

- Orbiting the Giant Hairball by Gordon MacKenzie

- The Fred Factor by Mark Sanborn

- Sell Different! By Lee Salz

- Sales Differentiation by Lee Salez

- Riding the Blue Train by Bart Sayle and Surinder Kumar

- The Infinite Game by Simon Sinek

- Start With Why by Simon Sinek

- It's Not What You Sell, It's What You Stand For by Roy Spencer Jr.

Also, don't forget to add your influences to this list as well.

See you next time! Until then You Never Walk Alone.

Made in the USA
Las Vegas, NV
07 October 2024

9809c029-edc3-4efb-9870-605a73957a6dR01